THE KEY TO HEALTH, WEALTH AND LOVE

JULIA SETON

Published by Left of Brain Books

Copyright © 2021 Left of Brain Books

ISBN 978-1-396-32057-6

First Edition

All rights reserved. No part of this publication may be reproduced, distributed, or transmitted in any form or by any means, including photocopying, recording, or other electronic or mechanical methods, without the prior written permission of the publisher, except in the case of brief quotations embodied in critical reviews and certain other noncommercial uses permitted by copyright law. Left of Brain Books is a division of Left of Brain Onboarding Pty Ltd.

Table of Contents

CHAPTER ONE. The New Revelation	1
CHAPTER TWO. The New Revelation	5
CHAPTER THREE. Health	9
CHAPTER FOUR. Health	12
CHAPTER FIVE. Health	14
CHAPTER SIX. Wealth	18
CHAPTER SEVEN. Wealth	22
CHAPTER EIGHT. Wealth	26
CHAPTER NINE. Wealth	29
CHAPTER TEN. Wealth	33
CHAPTER ELEVEN. The Use of Wealth	40
CHAPTER TWELVE. The Key to Love	44
CHAPTER THIRTEEN. How to Give a Transcendental Treatment	53
CHAPTER FOURTEEN. In the Silence	59
CHAPTER FIFTEEN. The Last Word	68

CHAPTER ONE.

THE NEW REVELATION

THE search of the race today is to discover the undiscovered states within the self; the new field of conquest is the conquest of the individual, and through this conquest to find new and fertile fields of power outside of the self.

The olden mystics wrote: "Get wisdom, but with all thy getting get understanding," and the New Age is to be one replete with full fledged understanding; "Back to the source" is the slogan of the New Age, and men know at last that within their own mind there lies, only half revealed, the true center of wisdom.

The new revelation shows that life is success or failure, happiness or despair, peace or strife, not by external surroundings, but through consciousness, either constructively or destructively posited.

The past, with its scientific, philosophical, and religious fundamentals, built a civilization which became the picture in form of these fundamentals; by these, the race has lived and ordered its whole existence; but in this modern rise of intelligence, many old fundamentals have been outgrown, while the vast majority of them are being shredded to fragments by the increasing intellectuality and spirituality of the race mind. Mankind as a unit is demanding a larger vision and a truer idea of life.

Mankind will keep for its use all that is best and holiest in all civilizations, but it will not fear to thrust aside half truths to grasp the whole, nor to reject that which is not fit material with which to build the structure of its new world.

The men and women of the olden world were human men and women, and a civilization arose to fit these states of consciousness. The race had expression only in the physical and mental sides of mind; man lived and phrased and objectified himself from the levels of consciousness with which he was familiar.

The new race is human still, living in a human world, obeying the laws of physical and mental being, but it has risen into the transcendental states of its own consciousness, speaking with a new tongue, a new language, manipulating its common human life with the laws of a superhuman understanding; living, clothing, feeding, and evoluting itself and others not alone through physical and mental knowledge, but from the higher states within which produce Revelators, Prophets, and modern Mystics.

The New Age will not *reform* man, it will *unfold* him and change him through this unfoldment. The new race consciousness is not based upon reform but upon change from the center.

The new race consciousness working from within, outwardly, will gradually displace the old ideas and old conditions. A new civilization must arise, not through strife, but through the finer law of mystical displacement.

In the new race consciousness men will not fight for their fundamentals or die for them, they will live with them ever alive in their minds, while with word, song, pen and brush, they sink them into the old race mind, until from the man with the hoe, to the higher illumined mystic there will come a subtle inoculation of New Thought ideals.

Out from the old civilization, individuals will collect together, in higher thought and purpose, then through collective individuality new cities will arise, and from these cities, new states, so that at last the combined influence of these collective individualists will control, direct and shape the American civilization.

Gathering around this higher law of civilization the expressions of human life will be different. The New Race will hold in its hand "the Key to Health, Wealth and Love and Usefulness"; the key to anything in life is only the *understanding* of its finer laws.

The New Race will be well, it will have everything, not through any metaphysical, mysterious, hidden method, but through sane, sensible, human laws, brought about and operated through the transcendental power of man's own mind.

The First Fundamental from which higher perfection will rise is the one of the *Atomic Mind* of *Substance* or *Universal Intelligence*. Man at last sees himself a nucleus of Mind surrounded with Mind. He sees every form of life as simply levels of mind made visible in form. Every manifested thing, even man himself, becomes a part of the one Universal Intelligence, everything seen or unseen, is simply a Kingdom in the larger Kingdom. There is nothing in life but spirit mind and spirit form; or *intelligence, force* and *substance.*

The mineral, vegetable, animal and human Kingdoms are as one great whole, each invested with the intelligence and form of its own Kingdom. The form of each is but a robe or material through which the centralized consciousness passes on and on to increasing levels of Universal mind.

Man is man, and not a mineral, nor an animal nor a vegetable; he has passed through these levels, and his consciousness is posited at a more inclusive level. He has thrown around himself atoms with intelligence attuned to the form of human consciousness.

Man looks at himself today in a new light; he finds that he is a composite body of intelligence drawn from the kingdoms through which he has evolved, and has within himself the exact polar opposite of everything that is without himself. He is the microcosm in the macrocosm.

He left the mineral only when its very highest law had been fulfilled and he took with him its master cells as the nucleus for his manifestation in higher form. He stands then, Lord of the mineral, for all the wisdom of the mineral consciousness is within his own body. He is the plus cell of this Kingdom.

He left the vegetable kingdom when the same law had been accomplished, then in the animal kingdom he passed through this same law of inclusion, and stood out in the level called Man the super cell of all Kingdoms through which his consciousness had evolved. He stands now, Lord of the mineral, Lord of the vegetable, Lord of the animal, while to this he adds the intelligence of the human level. He thus has formed a nucleus of power, making him Lord of all the lower kingdoms of consciousness, he becomes the *grand man* of the *Universe*, or a master mind working in power through, and with, all levels of the Universal mind.

Standing in this world of God Intelligence—(Himself a god) Man is the master mind in the world of mind, it is for him to command, every external thing must obey because he is positive in his consciousness to the atomic mind of substance, either singly or collectively.

The Mystic has written, "And God said, Let us make man in our image, after our likeness, and let them have dominion over every creeping thing that creepeth upon the earth. So God created man in his own image, in the image of God created He them." And again, "He shall eat of any deadly thing and it shall not hurt him." Why? Because the master cell of every Kingdom within himself, linked with his own human consciousness, becomes positive to the kingdom outside of himself; then linking his mind with higher intensity of Divine Mind, he can speak through his own consciousness as one having authority.

He turns to every Kingdom then, and his own master mind dictates what response he will give to this kingdom. He can, in truth, "Drink of any deadly thing and it will not hurt him"; he can stand in the center of the lions' den and he is their master—they must lie down. Out into the very mind of infinite ether, he can say to the waves and the winds "Peace, be still," and they will obey.

Man, as he becomes more and more familiar with the atomic mind, grows more cosmic in his own consciousness; he masters the laws of his own body and environment by simply intellectualizing and spiritualizing the intelligence of his own cells; by extending his mind to the atomic mind of the cells of his body, he regenerates, rebuilds his own flesh just as an architect can tear down an old structure and following a new idea, build a new and beautiful architectural design, just so, man can tear down his old body or environment which he has built through the mechanism of destructive states of consciousness and can fashion for himself a new flesh, a new environment, or both; and pass himself from a diseased body of flesh and a poverty-stricken environment into a body of health, grace and beauty, with surroundings of comfort and peace.

Each individual has within himself the nucleus of master cells which he derived from the Kingdoms through which he has evolved: His own mind, linked with these cells, brings him into at-one-ment within his own being making the divine wireless, and through this union into at-one-ment with all that is in the Universe. Then by intensifying the consciousness of his cells through the power of his own mind, he creates or destroys form at will.

CHAPTER TWO.

THE NEW REVELATION

SCIENCE has at last succeeded in teaching the minds of men that all substance consists of atoms of finer and finer vibratory rates of motion and that these Absolute atoms become localized centers in space, attracting other atoms, which, in time, become localized in form, thus giving us embodied universal substance.

Man, as we know him today, is the highest form of localized universal intelligence on this plane, a center of atomic intelligence. He is a specialized attracting vortex, and through his own understanding he may become a manipulator of all life's forces; he may create his own atmospheric environment and control and direct whatever he desires into objective expression.

His thoughts become the tools with which he reached out into formless, universal intelligence and fashions from his own atmospheric environment the things he desires.

If an individual does not know his own natural relationship with this universal substance, and is unable to recognize the Truth of his own power of personal creation, he separates himself from power and his life becomes the expression of the lesser things which he has fashioned for himself.

When he can be taught to recognize his oneness and go into the Universal Energy with the thought tools necessary to create, he sets this energy into action for himself. Energy set into action must become embodied; and since under this law it can embody only in man and his environment, the energy stimulated into activity registers upon himself and his physical world.

For those who know and understand this law, the Universal Intelligence has become a great reservoir or storehouse of formless substance from which the finite mind of man may create the things he desires; this substance is always waiting to be acted upon; man is the actor; his thoughts are the instruments with which he reaches out into its Atomic mind, and he creates through recognition the things which he holds in his mind.

No one gives to him but himself; no one takes away from him but himself; the infinite reservoir is always open; "Before you call, I answer; Ye have not chosen me, I have chosen you," is the promise of the ages.

Standing in the very heart of the Infinite, man has within himself the power to wave the magic wand of mystery. It is for him to command; he is the highest expression of consciousness on the earth plane; the formless, infinite intelligence must obey him; he stands on a pinnacle of supreme authority while the very silence around him whispers, "What is thy will?"

Jesus the Christ man taught us this sublime law. He talked with wind and waves as men would speak with men. He said: "Peace, be still," and they obeyed Him.

In this Universal Intelligence, there are four great levels of creation and all humanity desires to draw from these. If you could this moment hand a magic wand to every civilized human being on this planet and say to them, "Wave this, it will create for you from any level of your desire," there are just four desires which would take instantaneous form and these four great basic desires are Health, Wealth, Love and Usefulness.

No matter how we look at human longing, or study its material expression for attainment, we come back again and again for this truth; every hope, every emotion, every desire of the human mind, heart or body has its roots in one or the other, or all of these things; take any one away and life ceases to be perfect. Health, Wealth, Love and Usefulness, these may be called the square of all human purpose and desire.

There are three different attitudes which humanity takes toward this quaternary and the masters of the past said, "Know Ye not to whom Ye yield yourselves servants to obey, his servants Ye are"; and again, they said, "With what measure you mete it shall be meted unto you." The Universe is a mirror in which man sees reflected before him the vision of himself. His body, environment, friends, situations, all become the picture of his own conscious or unconscious projections.

There are those who recognize lack and have a continuous thought relationship with everything which makes for a limited supply of substance; this attitude gives them poverty-stricken environments and bodies. They have no idea of the psychological law of *recognition*. They know nothing but lack; they have a thought world of lack and have never known that they could say, "Let there be light," over their own manifested world.

Close to these, and only a little more emancipated is another great class; living about equally between lack and supply, they have placed themselves under the law of demand and supply. They build thoughts of abundance today and tomorrow spoil it by their thought relationship with lack. They have a degree of recognition of supply, but they have at the same time an equally active recognition of poverty. They want abundance to manifest for them, but at the same time they are unconsciously creating, through recognition, the conditions which must, by their very nature, divorce them from the things they desire. Some of this class really do not believe that they may have what they want, and I have heard them say, "I know I shall always have enough to keep me"; or again, they say, "I never expect to have many people to love me; if I have a few friends I am content"; and again, "I never expect to be real well, but if I can only have enough health to take care of myself, it is all I will ask." They are bound hand and foot by this idea of demand and supply. It has never dawned upon their minds that they are limiting themselves; they know they can have, to a degree, what they want, but they are careful to keep their *wants* inside the line of what they consider possible for them to secure. They have never dared to take their whole soul's desire and fling it out into the Universal Abundance of Supply, and to recognize its absolute fulfillment.

The third class, and by far the smallest number, have, through experience and observation, learned a great Universal Truth, that, if we want a perfect expression of abundance of supply on all planes, we must build a perfect recognition of these things into the great Cosmic Intelligence, and hold our life persistently one with this deeper law.

We get and keep and express for ourselves, in body and environment, whatever we have the power to create for ourselves in consciousness; supply is only a condition of mind. Recognition of abundance today, and lack tomorrow; perfection in one breath and imperfection the next; fear and anxiety, joy and sorrow; all these things will manifest for us in just the proportion in which we vitalize them.

Our *recognition* is our *Creator*, which fashions for us in the intelligence of our atmospheric environment the things with which we relate; and it is nobody's fault but our own if we do not like the finished production. We could just as easily have connected with every good and perfect thing had we known how to direct our creation intelligently.

Every life has a right to desire, and to have and to hold this quaternary for itself; no one says "No" to us but ourselves; The All Will wants us to have everything that we want, and will help us to secure it and aid us to keep it. The Universal Intelligence is no respecter of persons; and if we have lack while others have supply, there is nothing the matter with the Cosmic Consciousness, but there is something materially wrong with our comprehension of it.

Every human being on this planet is born heir to the best that the world can give, and when he knows enough not to accept less than his innermost desires, he can think his way straight into the center of Absolute opulence. "All that my Father hath is mine," the Master said, and he who knows, and who knowing, "never once forgets the pedigree divine of his own soul" can wrest from the universe without effort or price the substance which he needs in the building of his own perfected selfhood.

CHAPTER THREE.

Health

WE want health and must have it, because without it we cannot become perfect physical creatures and control and direct the changing conditions of our physical plane. We cannot drag diseased bodies with us on our journey through life and accomplish the great work of Him who sent us. The body must be free from pain and able to function normally on its own plane or we fail in the first step on life's pathway.

A sound body is the first requisite of a sound mind, and the first step on the path for the initiate is to conquer disease and weariness of the flesh. We must *see God* in the flesh before we can find Him in all the changing expressions of life around us.

Health is the first step in the quaternary; we may wait for recognition of Wealth, Love and Usefulness, but Health we must have, or we lag along the journey of life and defeat the purpose of our existence.

Health results from the operation of health laws. In order to have health, an individual must induce a health consciousness that extends through every particle of his flesh; this is accomplished through concentration, idealized imaging, and physical control, through increased mental power with sensible attention to physical needs. The body can be completely changed through these methods. The change can be brought about slowly or quickly, according to the individual's own efficiency.

Today we know that there are great Cosmic currents which make for Health, just as there are currents that make for heat, light and electricity, and that when we can touch these currents they rush through us, vitalizing and sustaining us, rebuilding our physical cells and producing for us new, healthy tissues. These currents of Health are capable of being attracted and localized in our bodies through our own deepening understanding.

There are within our bodies two great centers for the localization of this Cosmic energy; one is the solar plexus center, and the other is the brain, with its accompanying thought force.

Disease is the result of the mixed currents of the conscious mind, registering for a prolonged period diverse and negative thought force. Health is the production of the higher Positive energy registering in the body, a force that makes for strength and vitality.

When one has taught himself how to control his conscious mind and to declare just what form of the Universal force he will register, he soon passes his life into an expression of wholeness.

The individual who has perfect equalization between the positive and negative forces of his own being has health. Health and disease have no relation to each other; they are both the products of natural laws, and each belongs to the consciousness that produces them.

The first lesson to learn, in order to destroy the disease body, is to inhibit all negative thought. In some cases this cannot be accomplished without physical assistance; some individuals are forced to complement the change in ideas with a complete change of surroundings and friends. Friends and families, more often than any other things, tend to keep the mind in the old thought ruts. There is little hope of regenerating a physical body when the mind is allowed to drag on day after day in the old suggestions and ideas which it has built for itself and accepted from others.

The mind must first be tranquilized and taught to retain health concepts and then gradually bring these concepts into a perfect vision of health, and in time, join all the ideas into one perfect vision of health, then hold this constantly in the field of consciousness.

The real secret of health is revealed by awakening the understanding of the individual so that he recognizes and relates himself with the great Creative energy of the universe; he first learns to know from whence he receives his power, and then how to relate his physical body with it through his own mind and thoughts; his thoughts then become his Creator, and they create for him in flesh just the things he commands them to create.

The idea centers of the individual are the active agents of regeneration. Ideas have definite centers in the cortex of the brain, and all physical expression is brought about by this chain of cortex centers.

All mental states are registered in the flesh; grief, fear, worry, despair, anger, hate, resistance, anxiety, condemnation are all negative, destructive ideas. They weaken the idea centers of the brain, and when these states are persisted in they communicate themselves to the flesh until a complementary body of inharmony is established, which continues as long as the states of mind remain. To antidote this, the individual must raise his ideation and in this process he brings about a new cell registration.

In diseased minds the ideas necessary to create new physical conditions, or for the restraint of abnormal conditions, which are already created, are weak— sometimes even absent. Two ideas cannot occupy the mind at the same time, and the negative, unhealthy, abnormal ideas must slowly be crowded out and replaced by positive, constructive ones. It takes more than a few incoherent thoughts of health to crowd out the old negative ideas. Health will only come to the flesh when one has become able to build for himself a health consciousness, and a health consciousness is built through thoughts of love, peace, joy, nonresistance and tranquillity.

The full regeneration of the body is brought about through the daily renewal of the mind, and the secret of this renewal is through a contact between the life cells of the body and the individual's consciousness. The switchboard where contact is made is in the idea centers of the physical brain. Here energy is generated and sent out and the patient's effort is to get his "Idea switchboard" under control. He does this by beginning to centralize his thoughts and intensify his idea centers, thus sending strong, decisive currents through his flesh.

In the ordinary diseased individual the idea centers of his own mind are in wild disconnection and strife, while body, emotion and mind are in a state of separation. The idea centers and the body centers are driven on in a wild explosion of electrical energy which only over-stimulates and then paralyzes through over-stimulation, but does not completely destroy, while it defies the positive regenerative processes. Through concentration and control of his own ideas, the cells of his body can be subjected to normal changes.

When the idea centers and the vital life centers are in accord, the disease cells are electrocuted through the electric currents of the individual's own mind, and the life cells of his flesh build a new body to fit his new state of consciousness.

CHAPTER FOUR.

HEALTH

WHEN we have taught ourselves to recognize nothing but the strong, positive currents and ideas, and have decided that we will register only the force that makes us well, we come into a condition of thinking where the mind generates a vitalizing energy which reconstructs the whole physical body.

That health is a part of the Universal life, and exists to be used, just as do light and heat, is a truth that will, in time, be recognized by the many. But it does not yet admit to scientific proof sufficient to be brought to the minds of all men. With our present limited metaphysical knowledge, we can no more prove nor fully explain how healing is accomplished, through conscious thought-connection with the healing currents from the battery of life, than we can prove how the electric currents run along the line, nor how the blade of grass grows, nor how the red creeps over the robin's breast. But healing does come and abide with those who learn the power of this Cosmic union, through their own mind becoming a conscious center, and it hangs its signals of health on the body in signs too plain to be misunderstood.

We should never be sick, never could be sick, unless we had sometime, somewhere in thought, recognized inharmony in the Absolute, and then allowed this negative energy to persist for us until it registered in our form.

We first allow the recognition of disease to get possession of our minds, and then we hold fast to a fixed idea of disease until it manifests for us.

Sometimes we are born into disease and open our eyes in pain and suffering, because, somewhere, in our soul's orbit we recognized the laws of inharmony which could embody only as imperfect physical conditions. When we are born into an inheritance of disease we can be sure that our lines of life have related with those who have behind them, somewhere stamped into the Cosmic pattern a long line of perverted thinking and thought recognition of disease. Nothing happens; everything is by natural law, and behind every deformed hunchback, or diseased body, there stands the Nemesis of the negative energy which it has created somewhere and forgotten; but the Cosmic proof is indelible, and to the end of the chapter that body carries out the registration. "We come the reaper of the things we sow," and interior thought-force must—and will—in time manifest corresponding external conditions.

We connect with this life current, or we lose our connection, by the power of our minds; first, through will, then through faith and at last through consciousness. Our physical bodies are at the mercy of our thoughts; they must register the energy with which we connect and vitalize into activity; and if we see sickness instead of health, limitation instead of freedom, we drag negative energy into our beings and lift it into expression in our bodies and our environment.

CHAPTER FIVE.

HEALTH

THE ordinary individual seeking health comes to us with a false position toward the things of his personal life, which attitude puts him out of harmony with Life's finer relations. He has built himself away from the center, and is busy living under the conflicting laws of the external plane. The laws of this plane are change and decay, and at last, overwhelmed by an expression he does not understand and cannot conquer without understanding, he grows discouraged and exalts it into a position of power over him.

Disease can never manifest for one who consciously fills his mind with the recognition of the Universal All Health and the creative power of his own thinking; he who sees nothing but ALL HEALTH interiorly and then passes his seeing into his external world and teaches himself to look, with wide open eyes, into the face of disease, seeing behind it and around it and *in* it, the perfect *God-image* of wholeness, will become free from any disease with which he is related; and if he is in health, he will forever abide in the expression.

When we can displace the fixed idea of disease, both in the Absolute and the apparent, with the fixed idea of health, we have established our relation with the latter, and it cannot refuse to manifest for us.

When we teach ourselves to believe in health in greater persistence than we ever believed in disease, we polarize our lives in at-one-ment with infinite consciousness and we pass through life in a grand master position, whose every expression is one of perfect health, perpetual opulence and divine realization.

After we have seen the Truth of the Absolute law of health we must then incorporate this Truth into every act of our daily lives. It is not enough to *believe* this, but it must be *actualized*, for the law of life is certain, and as soon as one has born into his consciousness a perfect ideal, he must *actualize* it or he loses it. The penalty, most certain and sure, is that, a realization, not actualized, leaves us and degenerates our power of action just that much more;

our first step after realization of this All Health Truth is to pour it through every avenue of our daily living.

There are many who do not know that the little things of life are disease-producers, and that by the recognition we give them, we become related to the negative energy they represent.

It is not often that things within our own beings disturb us into inharmony; it is the way those inner things of ours are met by those around us, and the amount of self-expression our environment allows. This continual warfare, which is called existence, wears out the life that has not learned its psychological connections, and attempts to go on, unconscious of its finer relationships.

The sick are nearly always modern Don Quixotes, fighting a world full of their own and other people's imaginary troubles; they go out to meet these negative, destructive things; they really see them afar off and go and welcome them, and then sigh in despair when the full force of their relationship falls upon them.

One of the first steps in correct recognition for health and strength and power is not to resist anything; stop fighting; agree with your adversary quickly; let everything go, and in its own way, until you can develop yourself to where you can control and direct all things. There is no use running after anything; no use holding on to anything; in the last analysis, effort is not necessary. *Effort* is for those who do not know any other way, but to the awakened soul it is a fool's method which it leaves behind in growing consciousness.

We do not go with things which are distasteful to us, but we cannot gain a thing by resisting them. It was written ages ago by One who knew, "Come unto me and I will give you rest; take my yoke upon you and learn of me, for my yoke is easy and my burden light."

The important step for actualization is to get *Easy* in the every-day life; no matter what we are doing or where we are, we must know it is just the place we built for ourselves, or we should not be there.

No one is to blame for it but ourselves; no one put us there but ourselves, and if we do not like it, we can leave it, in just the hour we come into a higher state of recognition. We created ourselves, in our present relationships of body, environment, everything; through desire in the past we must kiss the lips of our own will today.

We meet "our own" at every turn of our path, and "our own" is just what we attract to ourselves through our own recognition. If we do not like our creations, we can recreate ourselves on the planes of a new consciousness so high that these old conditions will fall from us like a worn-out cloak which we unclasp and drop from our shoulders.

We can go right on in our present environments agreeing with our adversary, and, through conscious thinking begin then and there to build a new kingdom for ourselves; and after we have really vitalized it into life, we shall be led into relationship with it on the external plane. We then and there pass the simple act of thinking into a fixed power and build into consciousness, intellectually and spiritually, the body and environment we desire.

We know that the All Will wants us to have everything that we want, and we can get it just as soon as we are developed enough to work with the tools Life puts into our hands at birth. When we have fully decided this, we take our want of health into our soul and putting away care, fear, anxiety, caution and disbelief, we walk on each day in a calm, serene faith, doing with our might what our hands find to do, living in the Eternal now, creating our own through the power of intensified recognition, and never laying down our desire until it manifest for us in our material body.

We first get free interiorly from our old thought bondage. How can we ever hope to become new when we wrap ourselves round with the graveclothes of our dead yesterdays? *We cannot.* There is no use fearing anything; no use regretting anything; we can look right into our every action and love it and call it good. We did the best we knew how; if we had known better, we would have done better, and the dead past can bury its dead alone, we need not be forever at its funeral.

If we have done the best we know and in spite of this we get a bitter experience from something that follows, there is no use being morbid, discouraged and sick over it; all we need to do is to begin again, in the light of the higher knowledge that our experience has given us; each year of our lives will see us passing into a deeper and deeper comprehension. We have been told by the stages of old, "Blessed is he that condemneth not himself in that thing which he alloweth," and condemnation and resistance are at the root of every disease-laden body.

"We are not conquered till we yield, and yield we need not; not while God like mists from grass shall wipe the stains of our battlefields from every morning that He brings to pass."

We need to teach ourselves to look forward to each new day with a pure delight of living; we need to rid ourselves of every haunting thought of disease and lack of power, and to vitalize ourselves, outwardly and inwardly, with new motives, new hopes and new joy of endeavor. New courage, new love, new wisdom, these must become our Celestial creed.

We must learn to lift our individuality and hold it in such an expression of power that all men will recognize it and be stimulated by it. There is no such thing in Health, Wealth or Love as the utter sinking of self; it is not usefulness, but foolishness. We must first learn to be honest with our own soul, then we are ready to look some other soul in the face and be honest with it. "In all things trust your own soul, for this is keeping the commandments."

When we get health under this law of harmonious self-expression, brought about by union with the All Health Energy of the universe, it is built on a foundation that cannot pass away; we become healed to stay healed, and we go each day deeper and deeper into the finer Cosmic relationships.

Feeling our inseparable oneness with the All Creative Energy of the Universe, we "abide" in this at-one-ment, and we build for ourselves new bodies so vital, so vibrant, so alive with the Cosmic Energy of Health and strength that we send forth from our beings radiant energy, which not only gives evidence of the place of power of our own lives, but also heals and vitalizes those who come near us.

We are whole then, and strong and wonderful in our new understanding and beautifully human in our use of the laws; we are off the old-thought plane of disease and have passed with one long, conscious leap over the laws of pain and physical limitations; we see God everywhere and are healed to stay healed, for we are at home in the flesh.

CHAPTER SIX.

WEALTH

WE do not have wealth simply because at one point in our unfoldment we lack the understanding of the laws of wealth.

All life is law, and the price of the good part of life is understanding of law. Without the law of life we are only on the edges of living and are not in life itself. Jesus said: "Not one jot or tittle of the law shall pass away," and, "I came not to destroy the law but to fulfill it." Only as man can learn the law of his own life, can he work out his desires into perfect expression.

On the path of life, like attracts like, and men do not gather grapes from thorns. Some of the race are rich today and some poor according to the law they have set in operation for themselves and not, as the old world thinks, by accident.

Poverty and riches are no things of external chance or vague happening, they are the conditions we have fashioned for ourselves in our consciousness.

The New Civilization knows that all external things have their origin in the interior states of the mind and that interior recognition makes exterior form.

Poverty is the picture of one state of consciousness, riches the expression of another. Lack inside is lack outside, abundance inside is abundance outside.

The old civilization gave the race mind the idea of mind as a dual force with this duality always in opposition, one force acting upon the other. These two forces were called spirit and matter. The old civilization held that matter was always the slave of spirit, always divorced and eternally subservient to it, as well as eternally at war with it. It found in its scheme of the Universe that matter and substance were evil, that everything pertaining to them was in bondage and that matter was always matter throughout all creation. It held that spirit was finer force always existent as spirit, always good and always the expression of freedom and goodness. It was seen also that human life bounded by these two expressions of power was either free or bound according to the force to which it gave its intelligence.

Under these interpretations of life the race understanding sank into a sense of separation which could only lead where it did—into deeper and deeper confusion and ignorance of the real truth. As long as the race mind saw in matter something evil and something only to be condemned, rejected and despised, there could be no such thing as dignity for anything in its realm, and allegiance to the things of form and matter set the seal of damnation on those who were either too undeveloped or too developed to reject it.

With this belief in their minds and this deadening law of duality in their hearts, the olden races dragged on, ground to dust and ashes between the wheels of a law set in operation by themselves. They tried as best they could to be true to a false ideal, and generations were born, and generations died, fighting an objective fight with the things of the world in which they had to live and a subjective fight with their own desires and necessities.

Centuries passed and when the race mind stood at the very pinnacle of separation, one half worshipping the world of form and living in bondage to the manifested, the other worshipping the world of the formless and unmanifested God, Jesus, the Christ was born. He brought with him the connecting link which gave the truth of life so clearly that in it could be seen the unity of spirit and matter.

He brought the race a *new* idea, and he linked in one grand master stroke the whole objective world of form and the subjective world of the formless. He said in his words too plain to be misunderstood: "All that my Father hath is mine;" and, "I and my father are one."

He brought this message of *unity* to an old race mind sunken everywhere in its idea of separation. Only the really evolved minds understood His meaning, but He stamped His message on the hearts of the multitudes and for two thousand years it has percolated through the race mind and in the New Civilization of the twentieth century it is more fully understood and interpreted.

Jesus did not differentiate between the things in form and the things in the formless; He said: "whatsoever ye ask believing, ye shall receive." He knew that God, His Father, was All and that God had only one thing out of which to build the world and that was Himself.

He knew that all things were God's and that the race was in a world of God substance; that whatever it wanted or needed it had only to ask and receive, to seek and find. There is nowhere any history of a break in His own line of transference from spirit mind into spirit form. He stirred the higher etheric vibrations of spiritual substance and the waters turned to wine. He touched the higher law of the unmanifested substance down through the etheric waves; He fed the multitude, and projected silver into the mouth of the fish for human supply.

From the invisible realm of spiritualized consciousness, he brought forth visible form, and at His touch spirit became matter and passed into tangible use.

With this matchless picture of the Christ message, the New Civilization is awake in the higher idea of supply, and wealth is only a picture of supply the race has projected for itself from limitless substance.

We know that all material phenomena are spiritual arrangements within the consciousness of man and that everything the world calls matter is but an emanation from the one substance while the infinite is only in reality a symbol of the infinite.

The power back of the projection into form is *desire*. This desire brings it out into expression; desire is the prophecy of fulfillment, "As a man thinketh in his heart, so is he."

Supply is only a symbol of race desire and a medium of exchange which is used to give each life the fullest expression objectively of its subjective self.

Through race evolution there came about between individuals and races a legitimate exchange of these desires in form, one gave to the other something he had, for something he had not, and they soon found that the one having the most desires, had the most things, or symbols, of desire, and that having the most things, they could have the largest exchange.

So barter and trade and competition were born into the world. If one tribe had a large number of sheep, and another had no sheep, but owned a vast number of cattle, if they desired exchange they could express their desires in trade; and if two calves were of more value to the one desiring them than four sheep, he then paid the equivalent of his desire and possessed the calves.

As human desire grew more and more in its intensity, and the races learned finer and finer methods of expressing these desires, there came a race consciousness which knew nought but the desire to amass things in form, many desired only material possessions and sought only material good, forgetting that there were many forms of desire within the soul which had at some time to be expressed as they went on into perfect unfoldment. This is the state of consciousness in which the rich man who said: "I will pull down my barns and build greater, and there will bestow all my fruits and my goods. And I will say to my soul, "Soul, thou hast much goods laid up for many years; take thine ease, eat, drink and be merry."

But God said unto him, "Thou fool, this night thy soul shall be required of thee, then whose shall those things be which thou hast provided?"

"So is it ever with him that layeth up treasure for himself, and is not rich toward God."

Every one must come sooner or later into the soul consciousness which desires other things than the purely material, and when this hour strikes, the wholly material things will be dust and ashes in the life of those who possessed them these things of purely physical pleasure will cloy and the desire of the soul will be for higher and higher forms.

Centuries have passed, and centuries have come. The race mind has gone on in finer and finer concentration in its desires and finer methods of expressing these desires; until today the symbol by which men manifest their desires for material expression of supply has taken finer centralization. Cattle, gems, servants, slaves and so forth, are no longer bartered, but every human desire among the higher races is summed up and symbolized by gold, silver and greenbacks, and called wealth. This wealth stands as a line of transference between the man invisible and the man visible, and with it he brings around him and works out in form all the desires of himself.

Wealth is simply the connecting link between spirit mind and spirit form: a substance used by man; it is neither good, bad, or indifferent, neither high or low, it simply *is*.

CHAPTER SEVEN.

WEALTH

THE old civilization taught that all external conditions came as the result of external action and that poverty was the polar opposite of wealth and was the result of the rich taking supply away from the poor; it saw an individual's line of transference blocked by the greed of another. Through old-thought centuries the race believed this inversion of the truth and crept on in resistance, strife and condemnation, never knowing where to put the blame. From this false premise of reasoning there came all the tyranny and bloodshed of the past. But today a veil of consciousness has lifted, and the new race mind sees life in its entirety and not in the part. One after another of the old race obsessions are lifting from our belief and we see the deeper working out of the law going on everywhere in human destiny.

All life is a school and each life is in its own grade; poverty is simply the lesson of one grade, riches the lesson of another.

There are millions of lives on this planet today who are poor because they have not evolved to where they are able to conquer supply.

The first step in the grade for the poverty-stricken is to learn to conquer supply and this conquest is brought about not from without but through the slow process of awakening individual perception, which neither the race nor the individual can outstrip.

As soon as they have learned this lesson they pass on into the next grade where they learn how to use wealth, and their place is immediately taken by another learning the old lesson. Jesus said: "The poor ye have always with you, but me ye have not." He knew his place on the path and he knew the place of the poor.

The New Civilization knows that there are now, and always will be, these babes in wisdom who must be poor, and poverty will be their natural portion until they lift it from themselves by increasing unfoldment and understanding. We see daily that if we filled their hands with gems and their hovels with comfort, there would still be only gems in a beggar's hands until some stirring of deeper recognition went on within them.

Those who know life understanding *this first cause of poverty;* then looking more deeply they see that until the last man of this race, and of many other races, lies dead, the beggars of earth's supply will be in our midst, because back of the beggars' sores and hovels there is still the mind, the heart, the understanding of the beggar.

The second cause of poverty is the false education of the past which, instead of hastening race evolution, has served to keep it in bondage. The church for centuries has owned mind of the multitudes and the church has throughout all these centuries pushed the idea of poverty into the race mind and keep it there.

The church more than any other factor, has helped to hold the race mind in its bondage to poverty, for the church has held before the mind of the evoluting masses the picture of a Christ as a leader and an idealized object for emulation, and it has made this picture one of a bleeding, broken and poverty-stricken Christ-hood. It has distorted the grandeur and majesty of the Christ life and led the race mind away from fuller and greater paths of selfhood.

In addition to this Christ ideal of poverty, the church has pointed the race to their old God-head—a dual force—earth and heaven, and has given a mighty God and an angry devil, and all lack and suffering to this not too friendly God; it said, "Whom the Lord loveth, He chasteneth."

The old race mind was too undeveloped to think for itself and so for ages it lived by the thought-force of its leaders and men built their lives to express these beliefs. As long as men believed in two forces—God and devil—spirit and matter—they received these things, for "there is nothing in all this world but thinking makes it so." Held in the bondage of the old-thoughts and belief, men created and re-created their own lack, limitations, disease and poverty.

Under these teachings the multitude developed a poverty-stricken cringing consciousness, and everything in form being projected from the inner states of consciousness, it could not escape the law it set in operation for itself, and lack, crime, disease and hovels came the heritage of the race-man.

The race was taught that to be poor was to be spiritual, that it was "easier for the camel to go through the eye of a needle than for a rich man to enter the kingdom of Heaven," living in the lie of a futurity which they received from

St. Paul, they suffered on in misery, hoping and trusting that in some far-off future day, a heaven (if they deserved it by their faithful poverty) would be given them for their pain.

These old obsessions of race thought and race interpretation held the multitude in their iron clasp for centuries and strange as it may seem, even now in the very center of an enlightened century, there are still many minds hugging to their hearts this old delusion and dragging on in penury and despair, resisting the compelling force of higher revelation.

There are thousands, today poor, who still cling to this old tradition, only from false religious ardor and lack of self-investigation.

Another obsession of the race mind *is the one of inheritance.* It is yet said by those who should know better: "Oh, I am born to be poor." They are born to be poor only as long as they will not, do not, or cannot, learn the law of supply, and while there are many who are born to be poor in understanding, there are thousands who are fast working through their grade and are ready to come out into a new action of the law. The power to stand still under a law, or to go on into relationship with another is within the individuals himself, but not knowing this, he stands still, accepting an old condition as binding, when within himself there is the awakening power for freedom.

The New Civilization brings a new message and there are many millions in these days who are out into a new kingdom of thought, bringing new laws into operation in their environment.

We are poor and will stay poor only as long as we relate with the laws of poverty; success, wealth and supply can be planned for by every life just as scientifically as one can build a house or plan a city.

Supply cannot refuse to come to anyone who sets a supply law into operation; but he must be taught this law and brought step by step away from the old ideas and obsessions of the past into a new understanding and use of new methods.

Poverty and wealth are the results of interior states of mind and only as mind changes will material change.

There are childish states of consciousness which operate against material harmony; worry, hate, fear, anxiety and condemnation are interior pivots for exterior hovels and wherever man rests his idea and his energy, substance must gather round.

A mind that has been poised through incarnations in the belief of poverty and its power, and backs this belief in the present with childish of mind,—anger, worry and fear—will find poverty abiding with it.

Environment is only a big mirror in which each one sees himself reflected. A man in the bread line or who sleeps on the benches in the park, is doing so, not because circumstances force him to it, but because of his own ignorant manipulation of the laws, he has forced circumstances.

Lack will remain only as long as we have within ourselves the germ that intensifies it, and we will secure wealth and freedom only as we grow into it out from the natural states of our minds and hearts.

We are poor because we do not know any better than to be poor, and we stay poor because we are too ignorant, too weak or too inert, or, too superstitious to hold our life servant to the higher laws of life and compel a new physical arrangement, by an ever-increasing recognition of our God-power.

CHAPTER EIGHT.

WEALTH

IN the old thought method there are five ways by which we can get wealth and men use one or all of these at different places on their path, but there is always one of these ways which they intensify above the others and this intensified way becomes their line of transference, through it they bring to themselves the worked out forms of their desires.

These ways are: First, to *inherit wealth;* Second, *to attract it;* Third, *To marry it*; Fourth, *To work for it*; Fifth, *To find it*. These are all objective methods and belong to the age of objective individuality.

The first method is inheritance. When born into a rich family we become the inheritors of dead men's legacies; we come into this through the law of our own desire. Our ego has mastered supply in some previous incarnation and we chose to be born in at-one-ment with it. In such cases wealth and its conquest is not the lesson our soul came to learn in this life, but we came to learn some other lesson; sometimes the one of love, sometimes justice, and the use of wealth. This method claims many lives and it is one of the easiest pathways.

The second method, *attraction*—comes to those who have finished the grade of *work* and do not yet understand the law of active creation for themselves. Attraction is one of the easiest pathways to supply. Many lives are at this point of unfoldment and it is an accompaniment of the lighter side of labor.

There are many, who, holding fast to some work, attract to themselves the aid and co-operation of those who have conquered wealth and who have abundance.

There are two kinds of possession: One is passive, one active. Those under the law of *attraction* for wealth come under the law of passive possession; they use as their own the things which belong to others, and at any hour or at any place the owners can demand their own. So we find the lives under this law full of spasmodic possessions; they are up today and down tomorrow, until they learn to make themselves one with the law of active possession and create and hold their own.

The third method is a very popular and universal method. *Marrying wealth;* this is to some a noble pastime. The blasé nobleman marries the daughter of the wealthy commoner and completes his line of transference into wealth without effort. The whole trend of the old civilization was to this end; the entire education of the old-thought woman was to marry for supply; women for centuries have lived under the law of passive possession. The new woman will live under both laws, Creation and Attraction. The long history of alimony and divorces easily tells the story. Women have for centuries sold themselves to the highest bidder, and sold body, mind and spirit for supply. To marry wealth was in the past, and is now, on a certain level of understanding the principal occupation; it is not confined to women alone, men caught in the drag-net of this level of unfoldment do not hesitate to take advantages of this law.

There are thousands living in hateful environment and unhappy associations, because through this law of marriage they keep wealth around them. There are many at that particular point of unfoldment where they are either too ignorant, too undeveloped, or too lazy to walk out into their own independence. These tell their misery to every listener and if one asks them to come away from their old habits, they say, "I cannot," while some others look at the questioner and say, "they will not." But the new civilization knows that they cannot *will* to *will*, because back of their minds certain active ideas operate to bind them to the laws they have built for themselves; they drag on, getting the higher unfoldment through material dependence.

The fourth method is *working* for supply and conquering poverty through one's own endeavors. This is by far the largest line of transference and the hardest lesson to learn, but in this law everywhere the race works through the lesser levels of understanding and comes out into relationship with the law of abundance; with this struggle for existence there comes the development of many latent characteristics of the selfhood. To those laboring through the work plane, life seems hard and sometimes not quite worth while, but it has in it the germ of a divine realization which brings its own reward.

The last and least used method is *finding* wealth. There are many people who have at some supreme hour of need picked up wealth which some one had lost. Some lives have made their way comfortable with the amount they have found, but this is an uncertain method is only the objective answer to a great subjective momentary need.

Begging is also a means of getting wealth, but it does not exist as a separate line, it belongs as one of the minor lines of attraction.

All these methods were the laws of the old race mind, and they will continue to be for those who do not awaken into deeper consciousness.

CHAPTER NINE.

WEALTH

WE have a larger vision and a wider inclusion and the New Civilization sees all these methods as only lines of transference over which humanity reaches its own.

Inheriting, attracting, marrying, working for, or *finding* wealth are only material links between man and his desires.

The past races received wealth under these old methods and they took on the things which go with these methods—loss, contention, strife—but the new race is getting wealth over the same lines of transference and getting it from an entirely different center, from a new understanding of laws. The new race gets wealth to last forever and gets it in harmony and peace.

The old race worked with two substances, two forces, and had a world of objective and subjective power. They always lived in the law of separation and overcoming, and as wealth was matter, and wealth belonged to the devil, there was little joy or peace in the possession, even after it was accomplished.

If they inherited wealth they lived in fear of losing it again, or they lived in tumult because it might be diverted to other lives. If they worked for it they labored and repined and never were sure that work and supply would last, they were always in fear of losing their work, and with this a deadening uncertainty about their wealth. If they attracted it, they lived in the constant fear of losing the friend who gave it to them; if they found it, they never knew when they would find more; and if they married it they often paid such a big price of inharmony for it that it turned to dust and ashes in their grasp.

So life went on, driven to bay at every side, until at last, born of this conflict the deeper states of consciousness of man became unveiled and truth came out.

The New Civilization, living under a new idea of life, brings out new methods and more perfected results. We begin at the beginning of all things in form and here we find the Self, linked with the Atomic mind of Universal substance, we link our lives with the Universal law of supply, and then we only choose over which line it shall manifest for us. We can *inherit* it, and make it an instrument through which we have freedom to express our deepest desires; we can *attract* it, and stand forever beside the life that helps us put our own life into harmony and usefulness; we can *marry* it, and live with it in all the accompanying states of peace and power and love, making our own life and the life of another divine bliss. We can *work* for it, and with this working learn the thorns and heartaches of our kind; we can *find* it, and at every place on the path where our soul stands in deep need, we can pick up the answer to our prayers. We can do all these things only as we have found the law and worked out the understanding of the law which God seemed to have written in riddles in the past.

In the ages gone by, men did not know how to sail the seas, or tunnel the earth, or conquer the air, nor was there a Burbank to teach them the crossing of natural laws. As soon as men knew more, they expressed more, and today all these things are made plain. In the law of psychological consciousness there have arisen psychological Burbanks who are working with unseen natural laws, bringing the race mind out into new found expressions of conscious power.

We know that the consciousness of man is always united with the consciousness of God, or Universal mind, and that all possession in form comes through recognition in Mind.

There is a law of divine transference to every life and this is each one's own consciousness; no one need spend another hour in lack or need once he knows this law. His supply is only limited by his own power of manipulating the law.

Whatever is outside our field of consciousness, does not exist for us, and the thought of lack and poverty, and the recognition of wealth, cannot occupy our minds at the same time.

In order to conquer lack, we have only to build for ourselves a supply consciousness. Realization and actualization of wealth will not come through strife or force, but by subjective transference to the self through the power of the self; it comes to remain as long as the higher law of the self is fulfilled.

Fine psychiatry and not *exertion* IS THE NEW RACE method; under this method man works out his old laws of lack and comes into new expression of power. He gets wealth and holds it, for it is his own, projected into form through the extension of his consciousness.

Creation in consciousness is the law of the New Civilization and when man can create his own environment in his mind, he will not have long to wait before it gathers round him in form and it will grow more and more perfect, keeping pace with his ever-increasing understanding. Just to know the Law; get operation of the law, abide in the union of life and the law, and the work is finished.

The first step toward Wealth is *recognition of wealth*, or "creation in consciousness." Thoughts are like streams and each thought runs into its own channel and the mind that is given over entirely to wealth and success and supply creations, can have no room for the creation of lesser things. The mind must be taught to see opulence. There is no lack in the universe, only in the minds of men, nothing in the universe recognizes economy save man, and he only at one place on the path. Man alone is capable of personal creations so we must believe he builds his own laws and he either unites or divorces himself from his source. Wealth is a part of the *all life* and exists as substance and is capable of being drawn to anyone who recognizes it and demands it.

There is only one substance, and man differentiates this substance according to his own recognition. We can pass this substance into the everyday need, or the future expectancy. We can create every finite thing for ourselves in the thought-form first, we can bring forth homes, business, food, travel and education; every success and supply must come out in form if we have created it in mind.

God, the Great Universal Life, is no respecter of persons or demands. "Whatsoever Ye ask," Jesus said, and it is for us to decide and to command; the Atomic mind of Universal substance waits our authority; there is concerted action between the command of man and Atomic intelligence.

God, the Universal Mind, wants us to have whatever we want, and will help us to get it, and aid us to hold it as long as we want it; no one takes away from us but ourselves. As soon as we learn that this law *is*, then we must learn to operate and daily live in its operation.

We must first get the idea, then push it out in thought-form; as long as we only have the idea, we have only realization, but when we can pass the idea into a perfect thought-form and hold eternal allegiance to this vision, we are on the path to immediate actualization and the allegiance will bring it into our environment; in this land of make-believe we become as little children and a child is greatest in the Kingdom of Heaven.

In our consciousness we must see the perfect thought-picture of the thing we desire. Everyone knows what he wants, everyone has a divine image toward which he is realizing. No matter what our desire is, we train our mind to possess it instantly in consciousness, and see it perfect at all times.

Creation in consciousness comes slowly at first, for the ordinary mind has not been taught to hold a perfect vision; the old distorted visions of the lesser thinking will intrude again and again; negative forms must be displaced by the perfected form with which we wish to be environed.

There is not an hour in our lives when we are acting without a vision. We are always creating either the thing we want or the thing we do not want, and the New Civilization realizes the folly of creating for itself pictures of the things it does not want, which, when they appear, can only bind it closer into limitations.

There are some minds that are full of negative images, their whole field of consciousness is lined with distorted thought-forms of poverty and bad luck; shanties, hovels, misfortune, doubt and fear—these have been their daily projections and they have vitalized them until they materialized.

After we begin to create in consciousness, some of our thought images will be crude, but so are an artist's first pictures crude, but to those who really see the vision and feel the law, there is no turning back and there can be no such word as failure. Standing fast in an unfaltering faith, with the vision perfect in unconsciousness, anyone can drive the new creation straight through their old environment and holding it there, the Atomic mind of substance cannot refuse to produce around us in form.

Plenty of whatever we project, or make believe, must come out into form, our realization becomes actualization and we are then in our law of divine transference which no one can limit but ourselves.

CHAPTER TEN.

WEALTH

WE must fill our whole field of consciousness with the thought image of plenty; there is abundance of supply everywhere; all anyone has to do is to look with eyes that see, and he cannot escape the truth of the Divine Opulence. There are the billion, billion blades of grass, the profusion of flowers and trees, the timber, the mountains, the vast continents and mighty seas.

All nature gives with a lavish hand, and it not only gives enough, but to spare; it runs to waste in giving. Think of the million eggs of the fish that are thrown out to the one that is fertilized and used in the law of reproduction; think of the acorns, the nuts; only one here and there is needed for the greater law of continuation of the species; we see an utter, lavish giving with no apparent lack anywhere.

In all this universe there is lack only in Man and his environment, and in the animal world he has subdued and made to share his limitations; left to themselves, the horses and cattle grow sleek on a thousand hills. In all this great world of material form and, abundant expression, Man alone is sad, sick, poor and unhappy, and he, alone, is conscious and endowed with power to create a new world from the things he has in his possession.

Knowing this, we must believe he suffers from himself, and his environment can only be the embodiment of the things that he has recognized in the Universal and worked out for himself in physical form.

There is not now, and never will be, any lack in the Universe for anyone, except in the degree which he recognizes it as existing for himself. Had we known how to see plenty with half the power that we have seen lack, we should have displaced lack long ago, for plenty is registration of the positive energy of thought, and lack is the registration of the negative energy.

No life can reach this plane of seeing and feeling Opulent, and creating an Opulent atmosphere, by allowing itself to go in old-thought ruts where everything speaks to it of poverty and under supply.

We cannot create wealth by pinching our earnings and holding on in fear to the thing we have. If we have-only a dollar, and must spend it, we must learn to let it go as if we had a thousand behind it (for we really have when we know the truth of divine supply and consciously unite ourselves with it). When we do not have this interior consciousness and try to spend our last cent, and instead of being Opulent we have the hearts of cowards and beggars, we had better hold on to it, for no more dollars will come when we send it over such lines of connections.

The thing we fear always comes upon us; fear is just as direct a line of relationship as love; it is not the amount we spend that counts, but the way in which we spend it. When we can spend our last dollar KNOWING, interiorly, that it is impossible for us to become penniless, we then get a position which will not only let that dollar go, but will bring us another over the same line of transference.

When a man is alone in a strange city and looks into his pocket-book and finds not a penny, the way to keep it empty is to recognize this lack and become paralyzed with fear and anxiety for the morrow.

Most people do this without knowing the laws they are setting into motion, their very recognition establishes their relationship with the things they do not want.

When we teach ourselves to look into an empty purse with the same feeling of Opulence that we should have if we saw a thousand dollars in it, then we have laid hold of the Energy that creates, and no power on earth can prevail to keep that purse empty. It is not in the *doing*, but in the "being Opulent" that we get the power, we must know how to look back of the things created (dollars, dimes and nickels) into the energy that creates, and this recognition held steadfastly, brings life into relation with higher lines of attraction.

When we can fully and actually incorporate into our minds the consciousness of infinite supply, and our inseparable connection with it, we may let go everything we have in the world and make instantaneous relation with the lines that will lead us again into abundance.

This does not mean that everyone can sit down with his hands folded and expect miracles to be performed for him; money does not manifest without material lines of transference.

We have to know how to go *deeply* into the Cosmic consciousness, in perfect at-one-ment, before we can do all the work of the external plane, through the interior law of recognition.

When we know the truth well enough, we need never do anything on the physical plane, for "the unseen things are the real things"; but until we come to this point of Knowing, we can go on fearlessly in any condition in which we find ourselves; we can take up any line that is congenial to us, and over the lines with which we connect materially, there passes back to us the abundant supply.

There are two avenues of transference to every life; one is the plane of competition and the other the plane of divine transference.

Those who come into the abundance of supply, come under the laws of the plane of divine transference and his banker is Universal Mind; those who recognize lack and limited supply are on the plane of competition and their bankers are men often as limited as themselves. On the latter plane, this power of seeing Opulently is as exact a law as on the plane of divine transference; but abundance of supply on the competitive plane is spasmodic; one is rich this year and poor the next; there is no peace nor power of possession; but under the law of Divine Transference we get, we have and we hold forever.

The plane of competition is the everyday world of cause and effect, and the working out of getting and taking from ourselves and others; the plane of divine transference is the one of Universal recognition of supply, and the working out of our own and another's rights on the plane of receiving and giving. On these higher, spiritual and intellectual planes of consciousness, the lines never cross nor tangle, but each one runs directly home to the center of self and over the same line on which we send out our inspired desires, there passes back to us the answer to our prayers.

The plane of competition is where the majority of mankind are working; they are under the law of get and take, an eye for an eye, a tooth for a tooth; although two thousand years ago, the greatest of all teachers told them over and over the law of Divine Transference, and brought to the race a new dispensation of non-resistance and cessation of effort.

There are lives everywhere working under the old law of the plane of competition and sighing for the results which only the law of Divine Transference can give. They are like the chickens in this familiar story.

A woman who had a great love for poultry decided that she would go into the chicken business, so she rented a small piece of land and gave up her time to the production of the finest possible breed of hens. During her years with the fowls she gained a great deal of practical, even metaphysical knowledge.

In relating some of her many observations and experiences she said: "Chickens are just like human beings, they have the same desires and they make the same mistakes and suffer from the reaction of their ignorance just as we do; I never feed the chickens, but I find something to use as a lesson for myself.

"Whenever it is time to feed them I take a huge pan full of many good things which chickens like and placing it in the center of the yard, call them. Some of them are near, some of them are far away, but at the sound of my voice and call, they all come running 'pell mell.' Some of the hens which are nearest the pan, grab a mouthful out of it and run away toward the corner of the yard, and others seeing them with a piece of food in their mouths chase wildly after them, totally ignoring my call and the full pan of food just before them.

"Before many minutes all the hens are out in the farthest corners, away from the food, fighting, scrambling and tumbling over each other in their attempts to secure the morsel which was in the mouths of the few, entirely unconscious of the big full pan of supply waiting just within easy reach.

"Isn't this the way with humans? Someone gets a little supply out of the great Universal pan and then the blind beside them begin to struggle with them to get possession of their little bit without going straight to the Universal source itself which is always waiting, full and free for them to come and take; the Universal Good awaits our return with the same natural law that awaited the hens.

"When the hens got through struggling and no one had anything, the pan was still standing waiting to supply in full, the hunger and wants of those who found their way back, and I have to call them back many times before they satisfy themselves from the pan and not from the bits they wrested from each other."

This story told in her simple way reveals plainly the great metaphysical Law of Divine Transference and the plane of competition.

The plane of competition is the mental field of conquest and the plane of Divine Transference is the soul's place of dominion. The battle is always on between these two planes, until the life chooses which it will serve; and when it lays hold of the higher law of dominion, it sees clearly the pathway of effort from which it has evolved.

On the plane of competition everyone is seeking his own through externals and is always busy attempting to control and direct the external objects in his life; on the plane of Divine Transference he lets externals alone and goes straight into the energy that creates; he gets back of every created thing, and sees and knows and lives, in the consciousness of his own power of creation. He knows that every external thing is depended alone upon his recognition of higher laws, and that the external is always a lesser copy of the interior thought world; he makes himself the master of the psychology of action through his own thought.

It is true that man has to work with objective things so long as he lives in a world where they are, but he learns to live *with* them, not *by* them nor *in* them.

God gave to man a mind and a brain with which to manipulate these external things, but at the same time he gave him a soul through which to receive the stimulus of higher creative energy, so that his external human affairs might be the miniature of his interior world.

As long as we direct our lives by the stimulus we receive from things outside of us, and from people and conditions, we remain under the plane of the law of competition, and never have a calm, sure, serene control of life, for the law of this plane is change, and attraction never can become permanent for anyone working with this law.

There is no use denying the power on this plane of conquests. There is power, and great power there, for it is the place of the will action; but it is useless to think that we can pass ourselves into continued peace and plenty over this line of competition.

Fear, lack, worry, anxiety, loss, despair; abundance now, and poverty next year; friends this year, and loneliness the next; attraction to the uttermost now, and failure complete in a future time; these are the trophies of the plane of competition and the scalps that warriors of this plane hang on their belts we can see everywhere.

The hospitals, asylums and sanatoriums are overrun by those who have fallen on this battlefield of life.

These conditions are the natural results of a natural law and belong to the lives which relate with them, but they can never have a place in a life that has learned the law of Divine Transference, for such a life is the finished product of its own thinking and has blossomed into peace.

The process of interior thought-union is the plane of Divine Transference, and we come into possession, in the moment that we come into recognition. We must first *know* of the existence of the plane of competition and the plane of Divine Transference. Every life must learn this truth some time as it passes along in its unfoldment, for when it is ready to understand, it is brought face to face with someone who has graduated into this wisdom; or it is thrashed around on the plane of competition by its own foolish lack of understanding, until, in some hour of despair, its soul gets conscious control and shows it a new way; then it is born into union with higher forces and life begins to change for it.

Everything comes to us from the infinite; the very atmosphere in which we live is simply Cosmic Intelligence; it hears and answers us, our conscious call brings it out from its absolute expression, and our conscious thoughts lift it into material form in the external world.

When we know this truth of the Law of Divine Transference, we just lift our minds above the thought world of effort and resistance, high above the planes of recognition of competition; we neither know or care what the external conditions may be; we only *Know* what we want, and know how, and when, and where, we want it and remember that "All that my Father hath is mine."

We forget that there is any condition that might have power over us; we know that the All Will wants us to have what we want, and we know that it is waiting for us in the creative Energy, ready to burst into bloom for us the moment we make continuous connection with it. God has provided some better things for us, and through us they can be made perfect.

When we get this New Thought Position and have a business, it will increase along every line. If we want a new position or want to change our present work, we are so full of the knowledge of our own power and the abundant supply of everything that we want, that when we go out to ask for one thing, a dozen other things come along with it, just because we are so full of a divine attraction which our conscious recognition has built into our life.

We know, then, that the thing we seek is seeking us, and we go out to meet it, fully expecting to see it meet us half-way. Then over our own external line of connection our abundance comes. We may inherit it, attract it, marry it, work for it—but come it must, and over any line we declare for ourselves, it is for us to command, form must obey.

In this new line of transference we never take anything from another, for we cannot do that anyway; even on the plane of competition, the law is that the thing we seek and our point of attraction must be equal, or it passes us and cleaves to the one who is strong enough to claim it physically, mentally or ethically. But under this higher law of recognition the lines never cross; everything finds its own place, and we get all the thing on a plane of consciousness so high that we have undisputed possession of it.

When we first come into the law of this plane of Divine Transference, we feel as if we were magnets attracting to us, from an unlimited source, these things we desire; but after awhile even this much separation ceases and we feel that we are the *abundance* itself, the *law* and the *Transference*. We are It, *All in All*, and are out into the kingdom of Cosmic dominion; our whole world environment becomes the picture of the wealth and abundance which we have earned for ourselves by our deepened consciousness.

We let go longings, hopings, fearings and anxieties and just become one in realization with the abundance of Universal supply; this must end for us in actualization on our material plane.

This is the great Cosmic Law from which there is no appeal. When we make our whole attitude, one of divine recognition of opulence, everything we desire will come from out the external world around us and attach itself to our lives, and we shall express the fullness of peace and power and plenty. We cease then to look to men, but rather to substance itself for our supply. Men may refuse to pay, but the law of supply never refuses; it pays today, tomorrow and forever, men must pay, when the *law* has spoken.

CHAPTER ELEVEN.

THE USE OF WEALTH

AFTER the race has learned the law of conquest of wealth, or material freedom, there remains still one more grade to make. This is the use of *Wealth* and the law of harmonious, constructive distribution of the things it has the power to create for itself.

The New Civilization sees the deeper psychology of race unfoldment and teaches from the deeper laws of race evolution. The lesson of getting wealth is only one more of the many lessons we are all learning and after we have finished this, we have yet to learn how to use our own creations.

There are many thousands who do not understand or master the law of getting Wealth, and there are just as many who, after having gotten it, have not learned the law of constructive use; they are yet babes in the use of their abundance. Opposed to these there are glorified rich men and women in every race and every country, who are using their wealth for God, for man and for themselves, and their gigantic monuments of helpfulness are unveiled hourly in the benediction given them by the loving hearts they have rescued from the lower levels of living.

There are two laws under which the race operates the use of wealth. One is the personal, the other the Universal, and everyone passes through the personal life first and comes by the law of transmutation into the Universal one.

Wealth gives everyone the privilege of working out himself, and in the first development, human life is always personal. The self is always uppermost at the personal place on the path and those who come into possession of wealth in the self-consciousness, use it for the self.

Jesus said: "It is easier for a camel to go through the eye of a needle than for a rich man to enter into the Kingdom of Heaven." He knew that a mind anchored in the pursuit of the wholly material idea would not be materializing the interior states of desire, and He knew that Heaven is self-harmony, for He said: "The Kingdom of Heaven is within you." He knew that no harmony can come until life has balanced its forces with universal laws.

Selfishness always means inharmony because it means separateness, not unity; those who have wealth and are using it for purely personal aggrandizement, are only students in the great life class in which wealth becomes their teacher, and through the reaction of the personal laws which they throw down upon themselves they learn their lessons and find the cure of the thing in the thing itself.

We are all engaged in just one work in the world and that is trying to express ourselves. The personal minds are always selfish in their first expressions; they set their own pace for self-expression. With the wealth they have created, they absolutely compel other weaker thinkers to follow their plan. Unless we know where we stand in our own minds, there is no chance of escaping being used by them, and as long as the race is not anchored on its own understanding, this "using" is all right, for by the constant friction it occasions within itself, the soul at last opens its eyes in recognition of life's finer laws, and its own higher selfhood, and takes its first step toward self-preservation.

Everyone in the world is working consciously or unconsciously toward higher and higher expression of himself, and it does not make the least difference what anyone else thinks about his expression, the way may often seem a poor way to those of us who have been through those same methods, but, nevertheless, it is a good way for the one using it, and by it he is pushed on into fuller inclusion.

Everything in the world is legitimate material for our use, we may use just as much or as little as we know how to use. If we are inclined by our lack of knowledge and selfishness to use things destructively, the Universal law takes its own time to fix its adjustments. "The mills of the Gods grind slowly, but they grind exceedingly small," and some day we meet ourself and settle the debt with our own coin. On the path of life, all forces must be equalized—if we sow the wind we reap the whirlwind.

There is a part of the race which allows itself to be used past the point of psychological tolerance, on the personal plane of action, and this is the only way by which the finer forces of their own consciousness can be mined out.

The personal life leads everyone from experience to experience, and these experiences become so intermingled with others' experiences, that humanity is everywhere bound together in the one great personal law, and it pays, and is paid, in its own coin.

Whatever anyone needs for his next step in unfoldment, desire drives him on to find, and he is answerable to himself and God only for his selection. Back of all action is desire, and back of all desire is necessity.

At one point on the path, the hearts of men will seek satisfaction through personal selfishness and exaltation of the Ego. Personal human desires are bounded more or less by pain, loss, disappointment, and the heart-break of life, but all these form the ladder by which we climb past our dead selves to higher things. All these separate, personal satisfactions are the flowers of the three of life whose root is *Truth*.

The Universal use of wealth includes the personal satisfaction, it means literally—seek first the kingdom of harmony and understanding within the self, and all these external things will be added—because they come as the result of our power fully poised, tranquillized consciousness.

In the true use of wealth we can have all our desires expressed to the fullest and live in glad rapture ministering to the need of others.

"The river widens as it nears the sea," and with our own life made powerful, free and unlimited, we can stand as a great revolving light for the darkened minds of the evolving multitudes.

We know what Wealth really is, why the race mind resolutely demands it; knowing the deeper laws of conquest over it, the higher uses of it, we can make our lives become pathways of peace, power and wisdom, over which the whole human race can pass into abundance of supply.

We can give of all we have, to those who have not; not "all we have," for that would again beggar us, but *of all* we have, and give without stint, full measure, pressed down and running over.

The new race mind is turning eagerly to be taught these new lessons and just as it grasps quickly the new method of conquering its own poverty, just so quickly can it be taught the higher *Universal* use of the wealth it has created for itself.

The New civilization will live life as Gods, fashioning their material universe; thought force rightly directed will build all the energy that creates, into myriad forms of created beauty, harmony and freedom; Man is now, and always has been the creator of his own material universe, he does in truth Know himself divine, and can live as an individualized God, on his own self-created pathway.

CHAPTER TWELVE.

THE KEY TO LOVE

THE reason we do not have love is because we do not know how to get it; everyone in this world does exactly the best he knows how, when he knows better he will do better—loveless lives have little part in the great Universal ultimate.

It is true that life as an initiation requires us to learn how to live alone, and not be lonely, but it should not take anyone a lifetime to get this lesson; the whole lesson of life may be in one hour's passing and not dragged through endless years of effort and strife.

We want love; nature demands it, for latent in every soul is the recognition, that love is the fulfilling of the law; without the softening and vivifying influence of love, all that is best in human expression sinks into oblivion.

The world has need of the lover, the Poet and the Minister; it has a great place for these tender souls who pass along with their very beings awake to the intensifying *one* power of life, in all and through all. The great healer, the great physician, the great actor, the truly great individual, in any expression of life, is the great lover.

We must have all this vivifying power alight within our souls so that, touch life where we may, we shall not sink down into the dull gray of the commonplace, and pass along with inspiration dead within us.

Those who have come into real Love never rest, for their whole life is filled and vitalized with a new power divine; they have heard God's call in the depths of their own being; they have within them from the first, all for which the rest of the world is striving, and their sense of the divine Love is so strong that it includes all humanity.

In the last analysis, all life is simply the call of heart to heart, life to life, Deep to Deep of being. It is truly said, "Love is the only thing that pays for life or makes death welcome," and those who work out in the hot harvest fields of human effort and human unfoldment must have their souls aglow with a divine compassion, that they may be able to take the hand of every faltering life that touches their own, and speak for it the words of Peace and Power and Love; speak them with such a strength of conviction that they fall like a benediction upon each discouraged heart, and aid it to turn around and lead on again to the hill-tops of a new, inspired living.

We must have love, else how can we touch those whose spirits are broken? And how else can we give them a sunrise of glory?

In order to find the key to Love, what must we know and do? When we come to the heart side of humanity, we again come face to face with the most vital question.

Everywhere hearts are laying down their idols under the mistaken idea of renunciation and building themselves with every breath they breathe, into the power of separation; the half of humanity really believes that old-thought nonsense,

> "One must clasp and one resign,
>   One drink lifes' rue and one its wine;
> And God will make the balance good."

This is the cry of the loveless all over the world; and when we look at those who have loved and lost, who have stood by the grave of their life's dearest hope, strangers to joy, peace and love, who have dared to live when life meant only woe—what shall we say to them? How shall we answer the question of Universal possession and point to the hilltops of a new hope?

The answer is not really so hard, nor is it impossible to understand, for there is a *truth* of love and of possession so high, that when we know it we look at life in a different manner than we ever could look at in the fog-swamps of the self-conscious plane.

We must learn to see life in its completeness and not in the part, in union, not in separation.

Under the law of life's finer relations it is not possible for anyone to lose his own; we always get everything that belongs to us, and when we lose a love, or fail to attract it, we have no right to it; we only return, or pass under law, the thing which, by the true balancing of forces belongs to another, Love never misses a life that has ever once connected with it anywhere in the universal balance. Many people have a thousand personal little loves, and these, embodied in form, come to them; but they do not remain, for the law of the personal plane is change; it is only as we develop into the Universal union that we find love on the planes of a consciousness so high that we have entire possession of it.

In order to get love we must give love, and upon our power of giving depends our love supply. There are some persons whom no one loves, they are Ishmaels, with their right hand against every man, and thus every man's hand is against them. They are turned inward, instead of outward, they feed on the conflicting emotions within themselves.

There are persons whom a few people love, but outside this little group they win very little affection to themselves. They are of the class who when he prayed, said: "God bless me and my folks, brother John and his folks, us four and no more." Their own love energy only reaches to the edge of the personal, they have very little radiation of love energy around them, little magnetic force to attract, they live and die in the orbit they have marked for themselves.

Again there are those whom everybody loves, even their enemies must admire and commend them. They are the friends of the friendless; they are the comforter of the comfortless; the companion of the gay; the entertainers of the dull, the altogether lovely, charming, something, which unconsciously all men turn unto. It is hard for them to remember when they were not loved; as hard for them to get away from the Universal love note, as it is for the other to strike it.

The way to get love is to give it, and true love is simply "understanding," when you can take time from your own personal desires and activities to find what another person wants or needs, feeling within yourself the very pangs of his own deep longing, then can eagerly, willingly, help him to get those things which will satisfy his soul and make him bigger and better for your assistance, you love this person, and by these actions have passed into true love; you love them with the love that heals and binds and blesses; such love intensified through many incarnations, becomes at last the Divine Compassion of the Master.

Every human heart needs a confessional; it must speak out its needs to someone and it must tell about itself to someone who will speak back in its own language; it is this deep-seated need of a confessional which has sunk the tap-root of permanency into the Catholic Church. God was too far off from

His own created world to hear our human plaints, but He could hear and answer through the medium of the great confessional Priesthood; this comforted the race heart of the old civilization until it could grow into a closer walk with its own God.

The one who understands us the best, is always the lover. *The perfect love of any life is that point of conscious union where explanation ceases*, "when I am with you, I am alone" writes one grand lover, "because you are simply a part of my being."

The way of life is joy, through love and service; we must give and do for others, not alone on our own way, but in the way they can receive and appreciate. No one can ever die alone who has lost his life in the life of humanity, for every bit of his long life of love-giving will come back to him in his closing days, to walk beside him and comfort his farewell to the world.

The human love in the form of the loved one, is the *True personal God*; the Ancients lost the true idea of the personal God, and mankind has forgotten the true teachings. Humanity and its old teachers have only the letter left to worship; "God is Love" they say, but they forget to see him in human form; even though the master said: "Ye neither know me or know the Father, had ye known Me, ye would have known the Father also."

They taught that love transformed beasts into men, but carefully turned the race mind away from the very God before them, to the impalpable presence of some unseen something which they could only touch in consciousness. The personal God become to them some far-off Majestic being, too high for human touch, and too cold for the warmth of needy lips and clinging caresses.

Today we find the personal God in the world of form around us; in the sky, in the sea, the trees, the earth, the flowers, the world of bird songs; all life speaks to us in God's own voice.

The "Little flower in the crannied wall" is only the face of God which invites our loving caresses; with the revealed wisdom of higher loving we can see that "if God is in the sea and sky and lives in light and rides the storm, then God is God although He be, enshrined within the human form, and claims glad reverence from me."

Many there would be who never come into the consciousness of the infinite union with their source, had they not found it first in the unchanging love of some heart, which reached for their own, and which had loved on through doubt and darkness to the hour of love's own victory. "Through light to love, through love, Oh God to Thee, how wonderful the way."

Tragore says:

"When I kiss your face to make you smile, my darling, I surely understand what the pleasure is that streams from the morning sky; and what delight that is which the summer breezes bring to my body—when I kiss your face to make you smile."

This is the celestial passion, which translated into human life, gives man the thrill of his own individualized Godhood.

So swinging around the long cycle of human unfoldment, we find today that the personal God has always been the human side of the divine selfhood. He is manifested in the sweet lips, the clinging clasp, the caresses, and the ever renewing love energy which flings each separate atom into conscious union with its own, and Elsie Barker says: "Truly He who worships the Father in the self of the beloved, has already acquired a soul," and Ella Wheeler Wilcox plusses this when she says: "Who loveth most, is nearest kin to God," and Christ the Great compassionate, who was all love or nothing, included all the prattling of centuries yet to be, when He said: "If you cannot love your brother whom you have seen, how can you love God whom you have not seen?"

There is a story of a woman who followed the old civilization's idea of love, and separateness, which tells well the story of the ultimate *failure*.

Filled in her youth with a great religious fervor, she followed the old idea, that to attach herself to the human side of affection would divorce her from God, so she slowly detached herself from every hint of personal affection, living in the realm of the so-called universal love, until she became the picture of her own spiritual isolation.

After years of service in her way, when she grew old, she found herself alone with her ideal, but deserted by her kind; she lived in a small village, no one in the village ever entered her door. As the years went on she grew more and more distant, and at last she was left to herself, no one troubled about her ideal; no one even spoke to her. She was left alone with her God and the earthly conditions she had fashioned for herself.

One day, after about thirty years of loneliness, the neighbors passing along the roadway saw crêpe hanging from her doorway, then suddenly they came from everywhere in eager sympathy to do what needed to be done for this lonely, solitary woman.

When they entered the house they were surprised to find her seated in a comfortable chair; well, hale, hearty and full of life. They exclaimed in amazement and asked, "But why did you hang crêpe on your door?" she answered: "Just to see what you would do if I were dead."

The newspapers commenting on this story said: "Isn't that just like the hard, selfish, careless world, to be so selfish and self-centered that a lone woman must hang crêpe on her door in order to get human attention or sympathy?" Yes, it looks that way at first, but if we look more deeply, we will find that it is a strange sort of individual law which will in any day or age allow a life to become so separated from its kind that it is forced to hang crêpe on its door to call to itself the aid and sympathy it is secretly craving.

The world is everywhere running over with hearts filled with longing. Hunger for love, hunger for sympathy, kindness, tenderness, consolation, everything begs for its own like the hungry eyes of a dog saying, "My share, please."

The world is white with service, but this service is not given from the mountain tops of spiritual loneliness, but out in the hot harvest fields of life where the needy walk alone. The Christ did not do His work outside of the multitude; while He worked for them, He walked with them; He eat with the publicans and the sinners, and healed while He passed in the throng; when He worked for himself, He went alone on the mountain top, but His great mission was side by side with the world He came to redeem.

Humanity calls for help through higher understanding, "hearts break in darkness, go, comfort them, go." Yet in the midst of all this great need, a human could exist who must hang crêpe on her door as a sign by which she could work her way back into human care and sympathy. Surely the great heresy is separateness, and those who follow it get the things which belong to it.

Today humanity is big and free enough not to sacrifice itself on the altar of superstition and tradition, and it knows that "as ye did unto the least of these, ye did unto me" is the full equation.

The veils are dropping from our eyes, and God in all through all in form, and out of form, is now the Truth of the real Godhood.

We can separate ourselves from our kind through superstition, tradition, or ignorance if we want, we can be cold, apart, holier than thou, or aloof, from a sense of fear for the consequences of promiscuous association with the masses, or we can be small and mean, fault-finding, and full of resistance, righteous and beset with spiritual pride; and each year the great hungry heart of the world which seeks its own, will turn away from us, and shunt us by leaving us alone, to eat out our heart, in bitterness of spirit; or we can be warm, sweet, and so full of love that we can see it in each atom's strife, and bend a loving ear to hear what all nature's voice is speaking, that, "All life is love, and love is quivering life," and this knowledge will wreathe around us and through us with such an all-compelling power that our looks, our tones, our touch, will fall like a benediction everywhere, and the world will come and gather around us, no matter where our feet may wander, bringing us the fruits of our life's greatness.

Love is an all-existing energy, like light or heat, and it is never the individual that one loves, but the sensation of active energy which that individual sets into motion within us. No localized individuality has in itself the power to vibrate the whole of one's life into a continuous activity, for there are manifold rates of active love-energy; AND IT IS THIS MISUNDERSTANDING that makes the world run after affinities; there are affinities for every plane of expression, but when a soul knows the great God-Truth, it finds that there is, after all, but one great affinity, and that is the consciousness of God in the human soul.

This is the Love and the Lover for which all life is seeking, and it is the highest rate of energy that can be experienced by the individual. The real lover of every life is God consciousness, and this consciousness is both formed and formless, and it is the desire for this that keeps the world of men busy in its endless seeking through form. God consciousness is the final destiny of every life, though often it is enshrined in a human form and claims glad worship until we pass through it to Absolute consciousness.

When a life has burned itself out with longing, pain, loss and human response to this love-energy, it turns back upon itself and finds its own; and then it is again back of the things created (the man or woman) into energy that creates, and it *loves love*, both in the disembodied and in the embodied forms of love. Then it stands with its face lifted to the kisses of the infinite, it leans hard on the eternal heart and finds the deeps of deepest loving, for it has married the man or woman within itself and become One in the Cosmic law of regeneration.

This is the marriage of the lamb, The Universal law of loving; and when a life knows this, it is never alone, it does not always ask for personal contact with personal affection; it gives love, it radiates love, because it *is* in itself love, but it is past the need or desire of localization, although localization follows naturally in its footsteps.

For those who do not know this law, there is only one method by which they may come into their personal possessions, and this is by creating the Love they desire in the Universal Energy and attracting the thing they Love to them through recognition. They must know, past all doubting, that the thing they seek is seeking them, whether they see it or not, and call to it, and it will come from out the silence and answer them. Ella Wheeler Wilcox tells the truth and the whole Truth in her story, "A girl's faith."

> "And so across the miles between,
>   As back of dawn the sunbeams play;
> There shines this face I have not seen,
>   Which yet will make my world someday."

Those who desire love must build it for themselves in the Absolute, and with the Faith that creates, see it approaching them. There is no fate that can keep it away; it must answer a conscious call, and they will really find it.

> "Will meet beneath Gods' arching skies,
>   stars fade out and shadows gleam;
> And looking into each others eyes,
>   Shall count the past but as a dream."

Again, for those who have stood beside an empty grave which has hidden from their eyes their life's dearest hope, this Truth of Universal Union is a never failing comfort; it is an unwritten Truth that consciousness always answers to consciousness throughout the whole Cosmos.

There is no death, no loss, no separation but in part. Our loved ones go on in answer to the laws they have established for themselves, and, higher than our human understanding, they are led onward into connection with their own; we lose their form from off this plane, for it is the law; but consciousness answers consciousness, and we may speak to them and receive our answer from the very center of the Cosmic heart.

Exchange of thought and manifestation of form are also possible on this physical plane, but they are abnormal expressions, and who knows the higher Cosmic relationships never relates himself with mediums of the other forms of physical and psychical phenomenal. "Blessed are the dead that die in the Lord (Law)," and in the law there is no mixing of places or currents, they are all one, but different in their expression, and each expression belongs to those who have normally connected with it.

The dead have work to do, but not here, for they have finished with the physical plane and are ready to go on if we let them alone.

The first to do is to take away from our minds any thought of separation from those we love; they touch the same consciousness, and we can feel and see them and know them; without physical demonstrations, love is here a revelation, not a distinct possession. We fill our minds with this great Truth, that what is ours we cannot lose, and if it has ever belonged to us, we find it again and again, in increasing states of consciousness.

It is impossible to think of loss when once the soul has sensed the truth of infinite union with the All Life, for to it, becomes only a little widening of lines, just a little farther reaching out into the Universal consciousness.

So for us "There is no sting to death," and for us, "The grave has lost its victory." "It is but passing with bated breath, and white, set face, a little strip of sea," to find our loved ones brighter, better than before, and our field of consciousness widened, our understanding broadened; and we have entered into the fuller joy of a closer union with the Absolute; seeing All, feeling All, being All; then we are free in an inspired world, and death and loss are no longer words of pain and mystery.

CHAPTER THIRTEEN.

How to Give a Transcendental Treatment

WE must go alone, if it is possible to do so, where we can feel the sense of freedom from disturbances   can give full surrender to the state of mind, thought and feeling we are going to induce.

If we cannot get alone in reality, if there is someone forever about, then we must try to go into the silence of our own being; stop paying attention to anything or anyone outside of ourself. We can go into the silence hanging onto the strap of a crowded car, just as easily as alone on the mountain top, when we know how, but in the beginning the student does not know how, outside things influence him, drawing him back to his surface thinking.

When we are alone, either in consciousness or in fact, then, begin to arrange our thought world through concentration; shut out one by one, all the old thoughts which have annoyed us, or those we have been in the habit of thinking.

We are now going to induce the state of mind in which we want to live; we must choose the thoughts that will establish health vibrations in our body, the circulation will release just as soon as we can establish the thoughts of peace, love, joy, happiness, health and strength in our own mind and hold them.

There is no use trying to go farther until we can pick up one big strong thought after another and hold it as long as we want to, just as long as an old worry, fear or anxiety thought can creep in and displace the positive thought, we have not yet established mental force enough to create anything, we will have to learn to play with thoughts as boys play with balls; take one up, lay it down, toss it out at will; take whatever we want in its place, before we will be able to make the cell body of our flesh take on a suggestion. We must have one big strong idea, two thoughts cannot hold the idea center at the same time.

Self treatment is simply psychological displacement, brought about by our mind. Since thoughts are things and create the things which are in our mind, then what folly to waste a bit of thought force creating anything that we don't want, no one wants disease, pain or poverty, and he will only escape these, when he learns not to recognize them in his field of consciousness, so, getting into the silence of our own mind, we begin to shut out every thought that does not link us with Health, Wealth, Love and Usefulness. We clean out our thought world and begin to fill it with the strong positive thoughts about the things which we do want, and which will make life for us the thing we wish it to be.

After we are truly the Divine thinker of our own thoughts, we can go farther; the next step is to build the perfect thought form of the thing that we want, and hold this vision until it comes out into actual existence.

The Health vision:

If it is Health we want we fill our mind with the thoughts which make for Health, we see ourselves just as we want to be, no matter how ill we may be; no matter how we ache and pain. No matter how far away from health we may seem, we never give this any thought, we just form the strong positive vision of ourselves in radiant health; we frame this vision in our mind just as the sculptor holds within his hand the vision of the figure he is going to cut into the block of marble before him.

This vision must be perfect in our inner consciousness, we must let ourselves stand out in mental form, strong, radiant, glowing with all that fine energy of physical force which we know as perfect health and strength.

This picture will only form when we have been able to blank out from our idea centers all visions of the old diseased personality, we must be so filled with this vision of perfect health in the flesh, that like the sculptor, we can stand before the uncut marble of our own flesh, and feel in it no power to drag us away from our immortal ideal of wholeness.

Working then with thought tools, a thousand times finer than the sculptor can ever use, we stamp this vision into the cell consciousness of our body; our cells are the creators, they create just what we dictate them to create, they cannot refuse to obey.

This picture formed powerfully, and held permanently in the idea centers of our surface mind will work itself out into the cell consciousness of our flesh, there is no appeal from this law; when we have trained our minds to think only the thoughts that link us with the positive ideas of all good and then merged all our mental force into one great focal point, the *vision*; there is no more chance for health of the flesh to escape us, than there is for the hand to escape the flame of a fire; this is divine alchemy. Perfect operation of this part of divine mind has waited for the rise of race consciousness to reveal it. It is one of life's finer relationships.

The diseased patient, poisoned by the discordant vibrations which he has let through his body with the miasmic laden thought current of his mind, can with this method clean out all his infected currents and build for himself a new mind and body, which will bear witness to this higher law by the signals of glorified health it hangs in his eyes and on his cheeks.

You cannot tell just how the red comes over the Robin's breast, nor how the blush comes into the heart of a rose, but it comes, and it comes from the great Cosmic forces which are pushing it out into form; just so the flush of health comes quietly creeping over the form of him who, in full at-one-ment with the Cosmic law, links himself with the One Mind in all and through all, then with his own mind driven straight by his conscious thought force, deliberately commands himself into perfected health.

How to treat for supply:

The processes of thought control are just the same as for health, but when the vision is reached there must be the perfect seeing of that thing which we call supply or wealth. What form do we want our wealth to take? Is it material gifts or mental or emotional? If it is material form that we want, such as a position, money, travel, home, study, change of scenery or environment, then we must let the picture of our desire form permanently in our mind, and live in it hourly, take for granted that it already exists; if it is a home that we want, we must just see the kind we desire and move into it mentally and abide; if it is a position, go and take it in our mind; if it is a change of environment, then while we walk on in our old conditions we just live and move and have being in the new conditions; we can live in a dream world made beautiful by our own inspired thinking; this will come out into form in just the degree that we have power to intensify it in our own mind and shut out from our idea centers the old conditions of lack from which we are rescuing ourselves.

Whatever condition or thing we desire, be sure that we take immediate possession of it mentally, spiritually, everlastingly, for all *things* are spiritual intelligence which must appear at our higher spiritual command.

With our mind posited in this perfect desire, we become a mental magnet attracting to ourselves from out of the so-called formless, the very things we have set our thought upon; this is creation in consciousness. The Ancients knew this law, for they said: "Man shall kiss the lips of his own desires."

When we have built the perfect vision of our true desire in supply and hung it in the field of absolute consciousness, linked with our own mind, then we are ready to go into the silence for the possession of our picture.

Wherever we posit our idea, and however, form or substance will gather around it. Plenty must come and abide with us, for we are one with the true law of Opulence.

How to treat the fulfillment of love:

The first steps are the same as for Health and Wealth, but the vision again differs, we take from our mind all thought of separateness and get a fixed thought of Universal oneness, feeling that all life is our life, and that there is only one man on the path and that is ourself, and that our hopes and dreams are every soul's hopes and dreams. We hold the desire ready to fulfill them, both through ourself, and through others, with no other wish than the one of universal union.

Then we stop thinking; at least stop all conscious thought and we will soon feel the incrush of a new tenderness. *Universal Brotherhood* is only higher unity with all there is within and without ourself.

This unity expressed in more acts of kindness, to the world around, will bring love from every source. We do something for somebody as quickly as we can and as often as we can. We turn to the first one we meet and find out what he needs, then help him to get it, this will soon pass into a great Universal love impulse which will drive us on unconsciously into the pathway of service, which is the pathway of divine compassion.

If it is personal love we want, we just build the vision of the love-one into the infinite mind, let this vision lead on, make it our love, that loves us and whom we love; we may make it purely personal and name it if we like. However, it is always easier to see just the perfect impersonal one, and let the true law of our love embody it in the form, which will bring us higher happiness.

Just hold the ideal man and woman of our dreams and we will find that in some unexpected moment he or she will come out on the path to meet us.

Do not forget that we must be the perfect mate of this being that we are building, and if we build a God or Goddess for ourself, remember they will ask for a God or Goddess with whom to mate. There are those who build their vision so far beyond the possibility of mating with them, that should the real vision appear, it would flee their path, there would be so little in common between them.

The thing we want and out own point of attraction must be equal and a God will not live or mate with a narrow tempestuous little creature who is at the best not yet a good human, and a Goddess will never stay long in the company of a man who has not sublimed this human life into the purified atmosphere where Goddesses can dwell.

With our own life lifted to the level of the thing we want, we can resolutely project the vision, walk on in conscious command and deep nor high can keep our own away from us.

When all our creation is finished, then we lay every thought down and prepare to go into the Silence. Up to this point we have been creating—and have learned that we must think, but from here we must know that we are the thinker, the thing thought of—and the thinking in one, and in this silence step into union with the energy that finishes our conscious visions.

How to give an absent treatment:

When the point of visualization is reached, instead of seeing the Self, just project the perfect vision of the one whom you wish to heal, strengthen, prosper, or comfort. See them in perfect possession of that thing which you feel is their need, or for which they have asked treatment; do exactly as you do for yourself and carry in consciousness the same divine desire for fulfillment, there is only one Self, and all selves are in It, "as Ye did it unto the least of these ye did it unto Me" the Higher Self.

Holding them perfected in the absolute for a few moments, finishes the treatment, then merge them with your own self into the greater consciousness of the silence; the Law has been fulfilled, the work is finished.

How often should one treat Himself? Twice daily; at night before going to sleep, in the morning before rising—the intervening hours are simply a process of abiding. If you can say, *I am* Health, Wealth, Love and Usefulness, and see the vision—then what is there to do but abide in this consciousness. *It Is*, then, let it *Be*!

Absent treatments may be given as often as the healer feels the *Call* for help; the patient always makes the demand, and it comes to the sensitive healer subjectively.

If there is no subjective *Chord* between, then three times daily, nine o'clock in the morning—high noon—six o'clock at night, are psychical hours when transference is easy.

Remember, it is just conscious immersion of the healer's mind in the One Mind. Conscious dominion of all spiritual forces within, and Conscious command of all spiritual forces without through the vision, then a silence, still as God Himself, and a *new* universe breaks into being, over which the individualized God Man can say "Let there be light," and there is light.

CHAPTER FOURTEEN.

IN THE SILENCE

IT is well to regard the silence from more than one standpoint of utility and to know that it is not only point where the concentrating mind cements, as it were, the visions which it has created, but also a place for soul communion with our source.

At some time or another in our lives we all come to a place where two or more courses open up for us, and we stand at the crossroads undecided which way to take. There is no friend near to whom we can appeal; it is here, that one who has developed the power of inner communion in the silence, can rest awhile and find *within* the solution of all difficulties.

This inner adviser has been named "The still small voice," "Our Guardian Angel," and many other symbolical terms which have served their purpose to awaken the race mind to the existence of an inner consciousness, but whatever we name it, it is that guidance we gain when we can subject our objective senses and link our divine mind with the Universal storehouse of knowledge.

There are many persons who know of and have proved this source and these have outgrown the books of reference and the advisers who have stood as their leaning posts of knowledge in the past; here is the place where all may, if they will, become at one with such knowledge and wisdom as could only be dimly glimpsed in the terms of any human language. Here is the source of ALL wisdom ever sung, written or spoken by the world's sages of all time and there is no deeper source. Higher than this no mind can go, and here is the level of uncontradicted authority.

Where do you go when you go into the silence? Not one in a hundred can answer. The majority of students think they go into some mysterious, unseen, unknown condition or place outside of themselves, which can only be attained by some abnormal process of thinking.

Very often the only place they go is "to go to sleep." The silence for many is only a place for a sweet little nap. There are those, who in order to defend their position, contend that they can get all the benefits of the silence in that little sleep. Don't you believe it; they can get the physical benefit in a way, but *sleep* is not *silence*. When one sleeps he goes into the Great Silence, but he does not get into the great psychical perception that the true silence brings.

The true silence is *waking sleep*, and man consciously puts his surface mind to sleep, then consciously awakens himself into a supreme activity.

The silence is an induced condition of mind and the only place anyone ever goes when he goes into the silence, is into the transcendental states of his own consciousness.

There are three distinct functions of the human mind and we must be familiar with these before we can understand our own psychology. These three functions are, generation of thought force, emanation of thought force, and reception of thought force; Generation, Emanation, Reception; this is the trinity of all physical, mental and psychological functioning.

Many minds are always generating thought energy, they never rest. They never really stop to take in a thought from another mind, or from the Universal current. The result is that their own minds continually eat up their own strength and power.

Others are always sending out thought emanations; they pass them directly into words, they talk, talk, talk, without a chance to consciously generate; they get brain fag from over stimulation of their generating and emanating centers. Often one can only get them to stop a moment and listen, by talking more loudly than they do, and at an increased word speed.

There are others who are always receiving; not in the true subjective sense of reception, but with their surface mind. They go about mute, thinkless, without words. They accept whatever is given them; the strongest suggestion is the last one they act upon.

The old thought mind had to be taught that it could think, and that it could generate and send out at *will*. The New Thought mind has learned that it can stop thinking and suspend its surface states of mind, and pass at will into the transcendental states of its own consciousness, and live in a divine passivity in the receptive state which it induces from choice.

The silence is simply the transcendental states of man's own mind, and in these states he finds that there is a plane of thought higher than thinking, which is registration, and in this condition he uses only the receptive side of consciousness and his own brain becomes then and there a wireless machine registering the messages in the Universal thought currents.

In this condition he becomes one with the Akashic records of the Universe and all that has ever been emanated, generated or registered on them is in his current.

The *silence* is the open doorway to Universal learning. "He that lacketh wisdom let him ask of God" and in this suspension of his surface states of mind, man reaches at length the *Great Perception* through the activity of his own receptive genius; as silence and receptivity increases, he comes to trust his own human mind to the uttermost, for to him, it is *God Himself* enshrined.

Many feel more in the Silence than they know. They pass the whole period in *sensation rather than in inception.*

There are many who cannot sit down to meditate, concentrate, create the vision, and go on into the wider reaches of their own mind without slipping into this period of sensation.

The moment they become still physically, and mentally, they begin to awaken to a delightful half hypnotic sense which steals over them; they neither know or care to go farther, nor do they desire to return to surface life; caught in this dream of the senses, they linger half entranced; often the awakening of the common senses and a return to normal active life, is accompanied with an almost perceptible mental effort; the lethargy lingers, and the quiet of sensation seems better than the realities of life.

This is not the True Silence, it is only one place on the pathway to the higher states; it is good to find, but those who linger here are but babes in wisdom, compared to those who go on and reach the tablelands of spiritual consciousness. This is not the plane of creation, or of registration, it is only the sleep state of the subjective faculties; just as the objective mind must be stilled and kept awake, so must the sub and supra levels of mind be dominated before the transcendental levels of consciousness can be attained.

When one reaches this zone of *sentient silence*, he must waken his thought centers again and come back to the level of conscious thinking and go out again into this sub-state, until he can pass with wide open soul eyes through the lotus land of human emotions within his own mind.

It is reached by the simple *knowing* that it *is* and a recognition of the subjective signs of the state; very soon one can learn to pass on, taking with him subjectively, all the luxuriant, subtle sensations of this zone, to mingle with the more rapid vibrations of the other zone.

Then with the surface mind and its thought essence mingled with the soft energy of the sensation zone, the Ego goes on and out into that limitless ocean of divine realization and illumination, where it is face to face with its God-self.

There are those who expect to get some wonderful physical or mental experience in the silence, they listen for some voice, expect to hear, see or feel some exciting sensations through flesh and emotions, and are discouraged when they do not, and think that they have not accomplished anything.

The true Silence is a state far above the sensation of mind or body; the mind and body are connected with concentration, creation and the vision, but Silence or registration is a function of the higher centers and the registration of Cosmic waves of force.

As long as one has not ascended beyond his immediate states of mind and feeling, he receives sensations and suggestions from them; but when he has suspended these states and come into communion with his supraself, he is in a condition of mind that does not register slower vibrations, at this point he should not see or feel anything, and this condition of *absolute immersion* is the *true* Silence. This moment does not last long, "A thousand years are but as one day" and a moment is as hours on these heights.

When he again takes up his common consciousness and functions through his brain and flesh, his surface mind reveals to him how far he has been out: body, mind, emotion, will then vibrate and scintillate with a renewed energy.

He has drank from the immortal fountain of power and strength and life more abundant is pulsing through him, but it is the surface mind that reveals his union and through this human sense he feels that in the silence he has been Identified.

Do not think that the Silence is a place for action, as the surface mind conceives activity. It is an activity so high that the idea centers fail to register it. Just as there are waves of light above and below the power of sensation of the retina of the eye, and sound waves below the registration of the normal hearing, so there are levels of thinking, feeling and being, beyond the normal sensation of mind.

Go into the Silence just *"to be"* not *"to do."* The doing ceases when you leave the levels of the vision, beyond this, the work belongs to the infinite and not the finite side of consciousness.

"As I am lifted up from the earth, I will draw all men unto Me" said the Christ man of the past; and the Christ men of the present and the future can only lift their lower, slower states of being into power, in the degree that they may merge them into conscious union with their deeper Universal centers.

In the beginning the student needs to be alone. He should have a time and place in which to begin his exercises. The first thing is to take a comfortable position, either standing, sitting or lying down, as may best suit him. He should then choose the attribute he wishes to develop and take from ten to fifteen minutes to concentrate on it. He should think of it in all its details; just what possession would mean to him; he should create it from the mental attitude of interior possession. If health is chosen, he should see himself as he would be. No matter what subject may be chosen, he should always see the perfect interior expression of it. He should never build anything but a perfect image, and feel that it is capable of being materialized by him.

The next step is to begin the inbreathing of long deep breaths, and at every breath he should feel and *know* that he is really drawing to himself from an inexhaustible supply, everything he desires; and he really is, for every material as well as spiritual thing is one and exists as force in the Universal energy and is capable of being attracted into being by those who can make conscious contact.

What shall we do with the breath when we go into the silence?

This is a legitimate question asked by many. In the first part of the silence one should take deep, long, conscious breaths. Breathing into himself the energy that creates the things for which he is concentrating.

In the second part when creating and projecting the vision, the breath should be breathed and a deep, rhythmical breathing established. A regular expiratory and inspiratory rhythm will help to perfectly polarize the mind and body.

In the third part, deep silence or immersion, the breath should be entirely forgotten and long, deep breaths usually result without conscious effort. The breaths are few or very deep and sometimes very far apart, sometimes two or three in one spasmodic breath.

It is not necessary to breathe much during the immersion period, as this period is the period of listening, and when one listens deeply, one cannot breathe. Everyone is familiar with the bated breath of the listener and in the stillness of true immersion the breath breathes us, we become the very breath of life itself.

After the student has concentrated and established a rhythmical breathing, he should feel that it is finished, and then proceed to pass himself into the great creative silence, where the thing he creates can become vitalized with an indestructible energy.

After we have built the vision in our mind, breathed and stamped it into the Universal Intelligence, our personal part of the divine plan of attainment is finished: when we have done our best, with all our might we can put our toil of God and He will finish what we have begun and more than that, there is a universal plus given to our vision which we never realized until it comes out in form, "with what measure you mete, it is meted unto you," and the universal mind keeps strict account and often we have built better than we know.

When we have finished the vision we can just fling it into the one mind and leave it; thinking on our part then ceases, it is finished in our world and whatever is finished in our world is finished in the Universal.

So we leave this perfect thing of our own creation for the Universal to finish and send back to us over the same line of desire which we used to send it out.

The Silence then becomes for us just another more intensified contact with Universal mind through our own super states of consciousness; we shut out from our mind all thoughts, even the vision itself, and blanking our mind, pass into a place of energy so high that thought cannot translate itself into form or words. We induce the sense of a great stillness and a white light; it may be that thoughts are still there, but we pass them by, and our mind refuses to register them just as a big voice will blur over a register that is too dull to receive it.

After while, a deep sense of immersion comes to us, we slip half unconsciously into a stillness too deep to even be felt; a little longer and the stillness has us. We are not in the silence then, but the silence is in us, and mind, soul, body and spirit is all in one great vibration blent.

This is the energy that creates and this flowing through the vision, the environment and the body pushes our new world of desire into form.

How often should we go into the Silence? When? How? These are the recurring questions of the student mind. New Thought holds that everyone should go into the Silence twice daily; in the morning just before rising, or directly after, and at night, the last thing before going to sleep. This gives the life a chance to get back to its source. Before contacting the currents of the day, and it can take out with it into its duties, the strength, poise and revelation it has included.

At night one goes out into the big silence of sleep, he should go consciously into profound Universal Union, knowing that unfoldment goes on in both the waking and sleeping states.

The answer to "How" is simple. Go into the Silence any way that is most comfortable to you. In the morning before arising, or after you awake, get a nice comfortable relationship with your surroundings and then go into the Silence. Some say that they cannot do this, as they immediately return to sleep. If this is so, then rise and get a comfortable position sitting; this holds true for the evening practice. If sleep is apt to conquer you, take the opportunity before getting into bed; but if you are master of your sleep centers, go to bed in the evening and send yourself into conscious union with your source, whilst you have complete physical repose and relaxation. If these hours are not possible, use any hour, time or place. The Silence is a state of consciousness, it is simply a new special perception.

The length of time is ten minutes. The steps are, meditation, concentration, creation—in consciousness, the vision, Consecration, The Silence (*or registration*).

At the point of registration, the vibrations are high, and a few moments do the work of hours. It is on these illumined levels of mind that creation is instantaneous.

Many people have been unsuccessful in obtaining the best results in the Silence and they often relinquish their efforts, when really this lack of result is due to many things which can be adjusted by the student.

In the first place we may be sure that there are no imperfections contained in the Law itself, for those who have been able to rise sufficiently in understanding are using the power it brings as a daily guide to their lives. We must therefore look elsewhere for the reason of our failure.

One of the first principles that must be learned if we are to gain our desires through Concentration, Visioning and the Silence, is *patience*.

There are many who have lived the major portion of their earth life, before the hour has struck for them to know of New Thought and the Great Universal Law which it reveals, and when this time comes, and they hear of the new field of possibility for man through his ability to build his desire by Concentration, and become one with subjective back of all life, in the Silence, they are fired with enthusiasm to have the Law work for them.

Many of these get no further than committing to memory the fundamental instructions of How to Concentrate, How to go into the Silence, etc., which are taught by the teachers of New and Higher thought, and only become faithful seekers for a little while.

These folk are like the gardener who planting seeds one day was disgusted that there were no plants blooming the next. They forget that all the old thought training which they have received from childhood, has been away from this teaching of man's divine possibilities, and they wonder why they cannot get the perfect at-one-ment which they are told is necessary to perfect realization.

The seed of the New idea which has been planted in their minds must be tended day by day; if they would only give a quarter of the time to the development of this new thinking that they have given to their "old thinking" they would know that attainment was for them.

Be patient therefore in your practice, for in the degree in which you are a patient and earnest seeker so will your attainment be.

The last words of the Silence:

The last step toward perfect immersion is to withdraw the mind from the external world entirely, relax and live in the full consciousness of power; this is accomplished by assuming a *listening* attitude. Get quiet—quiet—and still more quiet; listen—listen; this is the way to the center of being; listen—listen—listen; so deep you can hear your own heart beat. When you can hear the beating, or even feel fully the vibrations of your blood pulsing through your heart, you have come close into the Universal rhythm and are awake in the supra-consciousness of your own mind, and you are ready to make the great Cosmic union, and this union comes as a divine revelation; there is a tableland of the soul, this is it.

Those who touch it, know it, and speak its language; those who do not, can only read of it—and start out on the pathway of consciousness to find it, armored by the words, and guided by the signboards, their elder brothers have set for them.

Some day they will find it—enter into it—and when they find it, they will find what they will never forget—the voice of the Silence, telling them of their Celestial God-Hood.

CHAPTER FIFTEEN.

THE LAST WORD

THIS, then, is the key to Health, Wealth and Love and Usefulness; recognition first, last and all the time; the recognition of Divine Opulence and the everlasting abundance of supply; and the power to live, move and have being in the consciousness of these things,—the One Life in all and through all, that speaks its message into our consciousness. We have no sense of separation anywhere within us, for when we have come into realization of this Truth, life becomes one complete actualization; The Universal Cosmic Energy works through us as the current runs along the line, vitalizing and attracting.

With this Truth locked fast in our life, we do not grow cold or sad or selfish; we slight neither our own lives nor the lives of others; we are then in glad comradeship with everything in the Universe, and we speak to it as to a familiar friend, and it answers us.

We have then come to the great transmutation; we love the day, the night, every drifting cloud; every expression of life becomes more beautiful and full of its own power; every common law of life seems then the most wonderful and complete, and there is nothing our soul lacks or misses; for we are in conscious harmony with Energy that creates, and it pushes us onward with each passing hour into fuller and fuller unfoldment.

The knowledge of inseparable union, the prospect of Universal justice, the infinite progress before us in this New Thought comprehension, cheers and comforts us, and the light of the great joy beams upon us. We are always well and rich and happy and beloved, because we have made contact with the Universal joy of receiving and giving.

The promises of everlasting goodness, the gift of unfailing supplies, the glory of a love that never faileth, the answer to the staggering upward prayers of humanity. All the rest within our own divine selfhood.

Nations may come and go, wax strong and perish into nothingness, but, still higher than the changing Law of time, there will always be the voice of the eternal God-Truth speaking into the souls of men. Amid the world throng there will always be those who, pushed by the power of a glorified conviction, will speak again and again to the multitude the message Health, Wealth and Love.

Over all the seeming wreckage of our undeveloped years, and of our weak human understanding, this message will sweep into our souls and make us calm and strong, and uplift us to a great endeavour.

The voice of the Infinite is calling to us today, just as it has called to men of all races throughout all time. We know now, as clearly as in the past, that "No man cometh to the Father, except the Father draw him," and that just as soon as the human life looks up and seeks and asks, it finds; for the answer is already written, waiting for that one supreme moment when the human life shall come back to its Source.

In our everyday life, we must all forever pass between the world of sense and the world of revelation, and each life takes its place in, and works from, and with, the power with which it keeps itself related.

The power which gives man his place of sublime authority, is produced in his own thought world, and in his own human mind.

In the minds of men there is never a dawn of creation for anything except the first creative energy of Thought. Everything which reaches the human mind from the Cosmic Mind, is over the wires of transference of human ideas and human thought.

The formless cannot exist without the form; intelligence cannot express without embodiment; and the way it passes into form is through the creative energy of the human mind, united with the laws of objective substance.

Every life must, by natural law, live under and with these two forces—the formed and the formless. We come into form from the world of the formless; we pass out again into the world of the formless. The physical body at least, goes back into forms so minute that, to the common consciousness, it is formless; and the consciousness goes on into form too high for common comprehension. But wherever we awaken, we find ourselves face to face with a finite and infinite form.

When a life first finds out this great Truth, that it is between these two forces, it naturally follows that it feels as though it was only a random ball caught between them and tossed about like a leaf in a stream. And it seems as if, caught in the mighty current of the Law, nothing could stop its journey on into the great currents and whirlpools of despair, or on to calm rivers of placid peace and power. But at last, drifting from shore to shore, of the formed and the formless power, feeling the limiting force of the formed, and again touching the limitless outreaching of the formless, it sees and knows that it is a part of both, belonging to both, powerful on both, and it ceases its fears and tumult of mind and no longer asks, "God, what is man that Thou art mindful of him," but speaks in celestial joy, "I and my Father are one."

Whenever or wherever the soul awakens to this consciousness, it conquers the limitations of the finite law, through the use of the infinite intelligence, and turning in illumined thinking to the formed world, we find the promises that have been written there for us and we read the handwriting on the wall of our own lives and are alive in a new world.

As soon as the life finds all the power of the unseen side of its being, and links it with the All, it has made the atonement, the at-one-ment.

The great Infinite Mind claims every life as it passes on in its unfoldment. When we have developed within us this Infinite sense, we are then newly and powerfully awake in the finite, and at last see that ALL life is One—only that one is the inside, and the other the outside of human thinking.

The world is a field and each life in it is a tree, growing from Universal soil; only those will endure without becoming tempest-tossed by life's tempestuous rain and wind, who have the tap-root of self wrapped around the eternal, the changeless, and who have sunk their string of thought into the fathomless.

The currents of the great Life run through every human life, as the electrical energy runs along the wire, and this active spiritual force quickens all the energies of the human mind and soul.

Every individual life has all the universal life currents latent within it; and this knowledge, quickened through illumined thinking, brings forth the greater vitalizing spiritual power and lifts the life above the lesser planes of expression, placing it on peace-crowned heights of realization.

No life can hope to manifest all the energy within it, all at once, until it brings it to the surface through the avenues of its experiences.

All the latent energy of a life comes to the surface in just the proportion that the consciousness rises above the lower thought currents of the personal, limited self.

Everyday life, with its long train of human incidents, claims the attention of the multitude living in the objective unfoldment. The passing through these levels of thought is the pathway of every life. There are none who do not come this way, but the time we spend on each is of our own choosing, and today we know we may pass on as we become fit, and that this "becoming fit" lies with each one's own consciousness.

These higher laws of correspondence are always in operation in every life, and the moment any soul turns around and seeks communion with its Source, it is always accorded. For "As many as are led by the spirit of God (the infinite side of self, or the Universal Self instead of the personal) they become the sons of God."

The mind that is under the law of the lesser thought currents in the world, believes in the things of these currents; these *things* are pain, heart-ache, loss, separation, fear, despair, death, disease and poverty. They feel that they are alone in a mighty maze, where all these broken and destructive things are battling with them for conquest. They believe in limitation, for in this state of consciousness limitation seems real and fixed and never likely to be set aside. Not understanding the higher illumined planes of thinking, nor the power that is generated on these planes, they feel that they are bound body, mind, soul and spirit by conditions over which they have no control.

For ages there has been written above our heads in flaming words, a promise that never grows dim, "Him that cometh unto Me (the higher consciousness of the Infinite) I will in no wise cast out," and "God having provided some better things for you that they, without you, could not be made perfect;" and yet, blind with the tangled currents of our distorted lower thoughts, we could never see or hear it.

It is written: "After this I beheld a great multitude which no man could number, of all nations and people and tongues, which stood before the throne, clothed in white robes, and one of the elders answered saying unto me, What are they that are arrayed in white robes, and whence came they?" and I said unto him, "Thou knowest," and he said, "These are those which come out of great tribulation. They shall hunger no more, neither thirst any more."

For they are one with the *exalted* Law of human living, and are out upon the hilltops of a new found power.

This is the New Thought Truth of living: Any life, no matter where it may be in the lesser currents, can build itself away from the dark lowlands of human realities, into a new world of peace-crowned levels of being, through the simple action of its own thoughts.

There is no lot on earth so dark, so sad, so lonely, but when acted, upon by the illumined consciousness, it can be lifted away into new paths of purpose and endeavour. There is no such thing as *bondage* in the illumined mind. We are bound or free, sick or well, poor or rich, hopeless or happy, *not* by our external conditions, but by the *interior* condition of our minds. This is the message that the sages have sung for ages in every song and in every tongue.

From a bed of pain and conflict with the cruder currents of thought, the illumined mind can send out thoughts that can touch the very center of the Universal Mind; and over the same line with which it connects, there must pass back to it the higher energy of the radiant thought spheres.

From the very lowlands of human despair and human limitations, we can send our thoughts straight into connection with the source of all, and standing with mind and soul alive to the great mind, "every valley shall become exalted, every mountain and hilltop made low, the crooked way be made straight," and lo! the very path upon which we tread will lead us into actualization.

Crowned, then, with the joy of a deeper consciousness, we no longer mourn, we no longer falter, we have the key to the secrets of absolute creation. Life is real then, and whole, and powerfully complete, for we keep our human mind united with the Great God Mind.

We can find the tired, worn out, desolate world lives and lift them up, heal them, inspire them and transform with a new glory of being.

The one who has Universal Recognition never grows tired of his tasks; he rejoices in his increasing power to do, he sees the deep of supply that can be given to the deep of need which he lives to answer.

It is one of the comforts that the All Good gives to those who "seek and find," that they shall have this sense of peace and power and plenty with them always; our abundance begins in the very hour we sense our at-one-ment.

Health comes then because we have made contact with it in the absolute understanding—wealth comes because we have touched it in infinite substance instead of this same substance in form; our checks are all cashed for us by the Universal; man has become only the human Paying Teller.

Love joins us because we have clasped hands with it through conscious union with the All in All.

God is the name of love on our lips, and Love is the name of God deep hidden in the very center of our being,—and service to man is the highest worship of God.

Clothed then in rightness we walk a pathway fashioned from a glorified consciousness, and we shed our light about us as we go.

Health, Wealth and Love, Usefulness, these together form the soul's immortal song—and with these songs locked fast in our hearts, our today of struggling is over—the Joy of Divine realization *has come*.

These become forever our celestial Creed, and we can tell it with the voice of a master, no matter where our feet may wander. We are always the Guests of God; our steps are led through love, service and worship.

www.ingramcontent.com/pod-product-compliance
Lightning Source LLC
Chambersburg PA
CBHW020430010526
44118CB00010B/515